■ SCHOLASTIC

Classroom Management in Photographs

Full-Color Photographs With Teacher Descriptions
and Insights About What Really Works

BY MARIA L. CHANG

NEW YORK • TORONTO • LONDON • AUCKLAND • SYDNEY
MEXICO CITY • NEW DELHI • HONG KONG • BUENOS AIRES

Teaching *Resources*

DEDICATION

To Mom and Inay, my first teachers

ACKNOWLEDGMENTS

Many thanks to Terry Cooper, who took my idea for a simple magazine article and expanded it into a full-fledged book.

I'm very grateful to Shelley Harwayne and Joan Backer for putting me in touch with some of the best teachers in New York City, and to the teachers and staff of P.S. 1, 3, 41, 59, 111, 126, 234, and 321, for welcoming me into their schools.

Finally, this book would not be possible without Joanna Davis-Swing, my friend and editor, who encouraged me to finish this book; Holly Grundon, whose wonderful design makes this book so beautiful to look at; and Sal Principato, who worked really hard to make the photographs come alive.

Cover design by James Sarfati
Interior design by Holly Grundon
Digital imaging by Salvatore Principato

ISBN 0-439-53145-4
Copyright © 2004 by Maria L. Chang
All rights reserved.
Printed in the U.S.A.

8 9 10   40   11 10 09 08 07 06 05

contents

Page 13

Page 51

Page 73

Page 91

FOREWORD

By sharing her remarkable classroom photographs and the reflections of successful practitioners, Maria L. Chang has created a most valuable teacher reference. If staff rooms had coffee tables, this book would demand prominent placement for frequent browsing.

I must admit, however, that my first reaction to this book was, "The title just doesn't do it justice!" The photographs and reflections in this volume speak to so much more than classroom management. To me, having a beautifully designed, attractively arranged, and incredibly inviting classroom has everything to do with clarity of instruction, good work habits for students and teachers, aesthetic appreciation, provision of adequate supports, and pride in one's teaching and learning. In addition to acquiring management suggestions, readers who closely study the content of the bright and bold visuals will strengthen their abilities to create classroom libraries, match children with books, create purposeful word study activities, and, oh, so much more.

Teachers who have been privileged to visit master colleagues' classrooms will appreciate these clear and crisp photos, ones they wished they themselves had taken. No matter how many notes teachers jot when they visit a colleague, there is nothing like a strong visual to help an educator recall memorable images, returning to their own classrooms ready to imitate, innovate, and invent on their own. Likewise, teachers who have few opportunities to visit colleagues will find this book a true eye-opener, inspiring them to take a good hard look at their own classroom environments and engage in staff room conversations on the essential topics covered by Maria and the selected teachers, including: Setting Up the Classroom, Creating Classroom Routines and Procedures, Establishing a Learning Environment, and Managing Behavior. Then, too, reading the classroom teachers' own descriptions and comments should inspire readers to take a reflective stand about their own classroom environments, routines, and systems for organization.

Classroom Management in Photographs begins with the popular Frederick R. Barnard quotation, "One picture is worth ten thousand words." So, too, one carefully chosen classroom visit is often worth an entire workshop series, in-service program or university course. By providing us with visits to over 20 classrooms, Maria L. Chang has paid well-deserved tribute to all these hard-working and accomplished teachers, and for that the profession should be particularly grateful.

—*Shelley Harwayne*
Former Superintendent Community School District # 2, New York City

INTRODUCTION

**" One picture is worth
ten thousand words. "**

—FREDERICK R. BARNARD

When I started interviewing teachers about classroom setup and management, one teacher I spoke with mentioned that she would take pictures of other classrooms that she visited. "You can't absorb everything you see when you talk to a teacher or visit her classroom," explained Barbara Rossi of P.S. 59 in Manhattan. "So I take pictures of the room and keep them in a file. When I'm ready to set up my classroom, I look through the pictures for ideas."

That's exactly what *Classroom Management in Photographs* hopes to do—give you ideas on how to organize and manage your classroom by offering you a glimpse into other teachers' rooms. Inside you'll find lots of colorful photographs showing how accomplished teachers from New York City have set up their meeting areas, classroom libraries, learning centers, and other aspects of their classrooms, as well as how they facilitate teaching and learning and manage student behavior. You'll read about teachers' philosophies and see how they've applied their beliefs to the real world—their own classroom. Learn why one teacher places her meeting area at the farthest corner of her classroom, and why another makes sure her library is the first thing you see upon entering her room. See what routines some teachers have set up to make mornings easy to manage and to keep the rest of the day running smoothly. Find out what a "poetry window" looks like, how "word masks" help students learn to read, why a teacher divided her clock into quarters, and so much more.

The photographs here capture the best classroom management strategies of some of the best teachers in New York City. You'll find practical, easy-to-implement ideas that will inspire you—and perhaps spark new ideas of your own. Enjoy!

MEET THE TEACHERS

In conducting research for this book, I interviewed more than twenty teachers around the New York City area, most of who work in the well-known District 2 (now part of Instructional Region 9). They teach children from kindergarten to 5th grade, in both general and special education settings. Here are the teachers who made this book possible and their philosophies about setting up, organizing, and managing their classrooms:

SUK ALBINO
P.S. 126, GRADE 1

When children first enter my classroom, I want them to perceive it as an organized place and an open space. I think when a room is cluttered or crowded, it makes people feel cluttered themselves. When you walk into my room, your mind clears up because the room is open and everything is in its place, giving you a sense of calmness. If there are lots of nooks and crannies, it feels like you're maneuvering through a maze, and when you're maneuvering through a maze, you're not calm. You're wondering, Where am I going next? Anybody who walks into my room can see where everything is, so they feel calm.

ISABEL BEATON
P.S. 3, GRADE K/1

For me, children's health and safety always come first. So that means I need to be able to lift my chin from wherever I am, scan the room, and see everybody. I don't have any high furniture so all the work areas are clearly visible to me. The second most important thing in setting up a classroom is that the definitions of different areas have to make sense to children—they can look at an area and know what it's for. They know that this is the meeting area where our books are and where they can find things that they'll use for research during morning meeting. The dramatic play area has clear boundaries so children know where to stay when they're in dramatic play. The block area also has clear boundaries so they know where to build with blocks. The children know where everything goes. And from the first day, we live the rituals and routines that we're going to live on the very last day.

JENNIFER CHALFIN
P.S. 59, GRADE 2

I want my classroom to be a very welcoming environment, very warm.
I use bright colors to stimulate children. The room is organized in centers or
areas so children know where the writing center is and where the library is.
It's also important that there's enough space for children to move around.

By second grade, children really need to become more independent.
When my students come in the morning, they know the morning routine, understanding where to
turn in their homework folder and notes from home, pick up mail for the day, and so on. I want my
students to feel that they're part of the community and that they can help maintain the classroom.

SALLY CHO
P.S. 41, GRADE 1

When children walk into their classroom, I want them to feel excited and
motivated by their surroundings. I try to create a child-friendly learning
environment—a place to grow, explore, and take risks. In addition, I think it is
very important to teach children respect, independence, and accountability.
The children are responsible for keeping the classroom clean and organized.
It is not just my classroom; it is *theirs*.

ALLYSON DALEY
P.S. 321, GRADE 1

I want my classroom to be a place that reflects the interests and needs of my
students. When setting up in the fall, I place supplies in well-defined and easily
accessible areas so students can use them independently. Because we do a lot of
small-group and partnership work, I carefully consider furniture arrangement
and leave plenty of open space for my students to work in. Since I begin every
workshop teaching a mini-lesson in the meeting area, I need a space that has room for all my students
to sit as well as storage for my materials (i.e., easels, data pads, dry erase markers, charts). Having a
classroom where the placement of everything is both meaningful and purposeful encourages students to
use resources as needed and fosters a sense of community and shared ownership.

BARI FISCHER
P.S. 41, GRADE 5

I always refer to the classroom as "our classroom." I never refer to it as mine
because I want the kids to feel like it's theirs also. I want kids to feel like they're
walking into their own room, and that it's a comfortable place—almost like
when you walk through the door and you go, "Ahh...." It's a bit harder to make
a room feel warm and welcoming to older kids because they don't want to be
babied so much. In kindergarten you can put little kids' stuff out and they love that. Fifth graders will
protest, "I'm not a baby anymore!"

ORANGE GIRTZ
P.S. 41, GRADE 4

I view my classroom as a home away from home. At the beginning of the year, my students and I talk about the fact that they spend most of their day here with me, together. Given that, our classroom should be a place where they're comfortable and they feel safe. When they first come in, they notice the pillows, the rugs, the homey touches, the flowers. That's the kind of atmosphere I try to create. The classroom is bright and coordinated at the same time.

JODI GREENFIELD
P.S. 41, GRADE 4

I want my students to feel warm and comfortable when they enter the classroom. The room is their home from 8:20 A.M. to 2:40 P.M., and they should be comfortable here. I put pillows in the meeting area. Every day I have "Pillow People"—six kids who get to sit on pillows in the meeting area. I think when kids are more relaxed, their writing and reading is more comfortable and they get more out of it.

ALLISON GRONSBELL & JANICE KURZ
P.S. 41, GRADE 3

Our classroom is a mixture of general education and special education students, and we teach collaboratively. What makes the collaborative model stand out is that a lot of things in this classroom are very visual. Everything is very colorful and very organized. We label everything—students can see exactly what everything is. This gives them more direction. Another thing we consider when planning our classroom at the beginning of the year is making the room safe, comfortable, and open.

JEN HOPWOOD
P.S. 234, GRADE K–5 (SCIENCE)

My classroom is set up differently from regular classrooms because it has to be accessible to all levels of learning. Even though fifth graders come in here, I still need to have picture labels for kindergartners who more readily associate an object to a picture. Given the age span of the students I teach, I need to think a lot about what needs to be labeled, what doesn't need to be labeled, where to place things that I don't want kids to reach, and so on. I also like to keep my room pretty clean. When I was student teaching, one of my advisors told me, "If you're not going to hang it up at home, don't put it in your classroom." Anything that is up is matted and presentable.

RENEE HOUSER
P.S. 126, GRADE 4

Independence, function, and purpose—these are the most important things I consider when setting up my room. In addition to these: ownership. I put a lot of thought in planning how to set up my classroom so that kids can be independent. That's a big line of thinking for fourth graders in my school—organization and independence. But I also want them involved in setting up the room. I set up the tables and the meeting area, but I let students set up a lot on their own. For example, they organize the library; of course, I influence some of their decisions. I feel that if you let kids help set up the classroom, they'll take ownership of it and will take care of it a little bit better.

MIKI JENSEN
P.S. 234, GRADE 5

Kids need lots of space to move around comfortably, especially in the upper grades. Since we do all kinds of projects and group work, one of the things I think about when arranging my room is how to create an open-feeling space. To do that, I push everything against walls.

Management in the early weeks of school is more about creating a community rather than teaching kids how to use the meeting area or how to behave. All these kids are coming together from different classes and will have to spend the next year together. I spend a lot of time getting to know the kids. I think management becomes so much easier when you know your kids really well and when they know you really well. Those first few weeks are so important, because if you let things slide at the beginning of the year, then you're going to have to deal with it later and it will be a lot harder.

SAMANTHA KAPLAN-CITERA
P.S. 41, GRADE 1

My philosophy is based on independence. My main focus is to help develop independent learners. It is important to establish routines in the first few weeks of school so that time can be spent on instruction. Everything in my classroom is clearly labeled and accessible. During any given activity, we maximize the time available to us and work efficiently because of this classroom setup and the independence instilled in the children.

CHRISSY KOUKIOTIS
P.S. 1, GRADE 1

I want children to feel that the classroom is a place for them. It's a place where they can be very independent, and it's a place where they'll feel successful. It's also a place that I want them to create along with me throughout the year. Every year my room has been different. I've added so many more things to my room, and I think that's from getting to know the kids, getting to know the age group that I'm working with, and making the room accessible and child-oriented.

NAOMI LAKER
P.S. 41, GRADE 2

How do I want kids to feel when they first enter the classroom? I want them to feel that it's a safe, fun place to learn new things. Safe so that they feel comfortable taking risks, comfortable being themselves, and not worrying about whether or not they're good enough. Sometimes kids feel scared that if their work is not perfect, that it's not going to be good enough. And I would always want kids to feel that if they tried their best, then they're great. That's what I hope. And I hope that the room looks colorful and happy and inviting, and a fun place that they want to go hang out in.

EDGAR MCINTOSH & MARILU PECK
P.S. 41, K

We want the room to be inviting to students. We use a lot of color and student artwork to make it an exciting place. At the same time we want the class to be a very organized environment, a place where children can predict what's going to happen next. This helps children feel safe. When we think about behavior management, we think of it in terms of learning engagement—we want the children to be actively engaged in the environment and the lesson. So in planning our group time we spend a lot of time thinking about how to engage their senses and make things clear and predictable so students will really focus on the lesson. If students are confused or bored about what they are learning, they will eventually stop attending, and that can manifest itself in a variety of behavior problems. Our goal is to have a classroom full of happy, engaged students who celebrate the joy of learning together.

BARBARA ROSSI
P.S. 59, GRADE 3

I think a classroom should be welcoming and organized. It should be bright and colorful so that it's attractive and inviting to both parents and kids. And I think kids should feel ownership—it should be their classroom, not just my classroom. When kids enter the room, they should feel safe and welcomed. They should feel like it's their community; they own it. Independence is really important. When kids come in the morning, they should be able to unpack and put things away, know where everything goes, choose books, and say hello to their friends.

STEPHANIE SAUNDERS
P.S. 111, GRADE 4

I want children to walk into the classroom and feel like they're walking into a warm, comfortable place. But I feel it's important to get to know my students before I finalize a design for my classroom. I know that I'm going to have thirty unique students. There are modifications that I make every single day of teaching. One of the best things about teaching is that every day is a chance to start fresh.

JILL SIMON & JENNIFER GILLESPIE
P.S. 41, GRADE 2

Second grade is a huge transitional year. Some schools consider it secondary or intermediate; some schools consider it primary. That tells us that second grade is really like the transition between primary and intermediate. So we really want second graders to have independence. They are learners—they can learn for themselves, and they are responsible for everything that they do. If it's something that they can do themselves, we don't want to do it for them. Whatever the curriculum is, we want children to be able to do it themselves and have access to everything they need to learn and be in charge of themselves.

JACKIE SVATOVIC
P.S. 3, GRADE 2/3

My room is a place where children can come into and feel very welcome. I try to make it cozy like a home. I have a very pretty rug, a comfortable couch, and benches. When children arrive on the first day of school, I have flowers on every table. And very often, they start bringing in flowers too. This is a place that I want children to feel excited about coming to, and I think they do. I think they're so happy here, and I know I am.

I think the most important thing about a room is that it should facilitate children's socializing and make for community so that they feel invited into different areas to do things together. The children know where they can go in the room to do certain things. When children are engaged there's very little management needed.

CHAPTER 1

SETTING UP
The Classroom

> **"**Good management involves
> the prevention of problems;
> a carefully laid-out physical
> environment is the first step.**"**
>
> — JERE BROPHY & THOMAS GOOD (1984)

Open the door to any classroom, and you enter a unique space, the home away from home for students and their teacher. Each piece of furniture, each bulletin board, every bin and basket has been thoughtfully placed. Teachers pay attention to detail and orchestrate the physical components of their rooms to harmonize with the learning activities they plan.

A carefully designed room is the first step toward effective classroom management. In this section, you'll see how teachers from New York City laid out their rooms to reflect their teaching philosophies and support their teaching styles.

Meeting Area

"The whole-group meeting area is the heart of the learning environment, the place where the learning community is built and nourished."

— MARLYNN K. CLAYTON (2001)

The meeting area is the classroom's nucleus, where all students gather for morning meeting, read aloud, shared reading, mini-lessons, and other large-group activities. Often the meeting area is defined by a large, inviting rug and bordered by a wall, bookshelves, and a writing easel or chalkboard. Where you decide to place your meeting area will depend on the size and layout of your classroom, as well as on how you intend to use it in relation to the rest of the room.

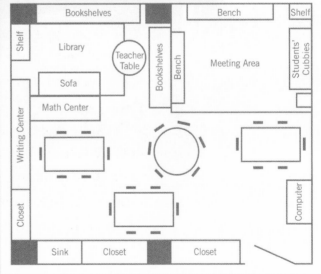

Teaching Central

The meeting area is the focal point of our classroom, the first thing you see when you enter the room. I set up my meeting area in front of the room because that's where the white board is located. Most of my teaching is centered around that board—our schedule is up there as well as my daily "do now" (a ten-minute math activity students do first thing in the morning), and I use it for my mini-lessons. I make sure my meeting area is the coziest and most inviting part of the room. We spend a lot of time here and I want students to feel motivated to learn.

—*Orange G.*

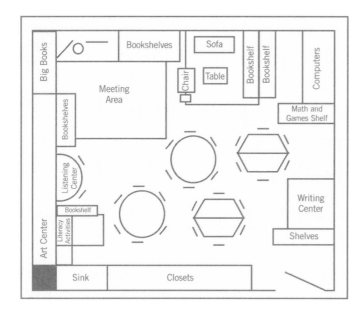

No Distractions

I always have my meeting area at the farthest corner from the door. I have the kids facing me, away from the door where they're not distracted. I'm the only one facing the doorway, so I can see if anything is happening outside. They don't need to see what's happening outside during lessons.

—*Suk A.*

Resource Area

My meeting area is bordered by the library so children can use the books as well as the print-rich wall for research during morning meeting. For example, let's say during the morning message somebody needs to spell *Monday*; he or she can look up the days of the week on the wall.

—*Isabel B.*

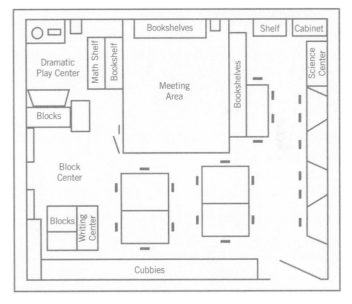

SEATING IN THE MEETING AREA

The whole-group lessons and class discussions that take place in the meeting area are vital to student learning; the right seating arrangement can help you make the most of this precious teaching time. Students need to have enough space to sit comfortably without disturbing their neighbors. Younger students can often sit on the rug, although older students may be more comfortable on benches or chairs. This section shares how teachers have accommodated their students' seating needs so that everyone can focus on learning.

Rug Spots

At the beginning of the year I let children choose where to sit on the rug. But certain kids could not sit next to some other kids so I assigned rug spots and put them on a chart for everyone to see. Their spots will change after about a month or so. I have three children who sit on chairs next to the rug—one is a student with behavior problems, another concentrates better sitting on a chair, and the third wears an FM system that helps him hear what I say. The FM system works better when the wearer sits at my eye level.

—*Jennifer C.*

Bench Rotation

I have benches around my meeting area because fifth graders' bodies are bigger than, say, third graders, and the space they require is bigger. So I bought seven benches and put them around the rug. Two children sit on each bench and the rest of the class sits on the rug in the middle. I feel it evens out the space more for them. I set up a schedule for who sits on the benches when. Students rotate around. On the floor, students can sit wherever they want.

—*Bari F.*

Lines to Sit On or Behind

For seating during my science lessons, I taped lines on my meeting area rug. The three lines create three distinct rows for students to sit in. The red line, the one closest to my chair, is the most important to me because it signals my personal space; children know not to sit in front of that line. The blue line indicates the start of the second row, and the back line (the piece that holds the rug down) marks the third row. Students in the third row can sit on the bench, or we might push the bench back and have them sit on the floor. Older students know that they have to sit behind the lines. But I ask kindergartners to sit on the line because they understand the word *on* better than *behind*.

—*Jen H.*

Double-Duty Crate Benches

I have crates for storing extra books and for kids to sit on in the meeting area. My kids are big and they keep growing. Sometimes it's hard for them to sit on the carpet, even though they don't sit there very long. The benches are just milk crates with wooden panels that I painted. Zip ties hold the panels in place.

—*Renee H.*

Pillow Pals

I put pillows in the meeting area, and every day I have what I call "Pillow People." Six kids get to sit on the pillows whenever we're in the meeting area so they can be a little more comfortable. I have a cup labeled "Pillow People of the Future," which is filled with clothespins labeled with the kids' names. Every day, I pick six clothespins and pin them to the "Pillow People" strip *(at right)*. At the end of the day, those clothespins go to the "Pillow People of the Past" cup. When the "Future" cup is empty, I put all the pins back there and we start all over again.

—*Jodi G.*

Bench Buddies

In our meeting area I have benches with colorful, comfortable pillows and a very inviting rug. There are 12 seats on the benches, and I rotate children every day using our "Bench Buddies" system, which works in the same way as Jodi's "Pillow People."

—*Orange G.*

SEATING FOR INDIVIDUAL NEEDS

Edgar McIntosh and Marilu Peck are collaborative team teachers whose class includes a mix of general education and special education kindergartners. To meet their students' individual needs, Edgar and Marilu offer a variety of seating arrangements in their meeting area. Here, they talk about a few options:

. . . To Get the Wiggles Out

" Some children have trouble sitting in the meeting area because their bodies are much more active than other children's bodies. So we might put a child in a red, bumpy cushion that has some air in it so he can move around and get the wiggles out while staying on it. The bumps help with movement. **"**

. . . To Keep Kids Awake

" Some students have low energy and need support while sitting. A sofa pillow with some cushioning helps a child who may have low muscle tone and might slump over or fall asleep. **"**

. . . To Help Kids Stay Put

" We put a carpet square on the floor for one child who tends to roll around without even knowing that he's rolled somewhere else. The carpet square defines his space a little bit, so he knows his bottom can go anywhere on the carpet square, but it needs to stay on the square. **"**

Seating for the Teacher

During morning meeting, teachers might choose to sit on the rug on the same level as their students. But when instructing the class, many teachers prefer to sit on a chair where they can see everyone and everyone can see them. Some teachers may also set aside a particular chair for special guests.

My Chair and the Share Chair

I have a colorful wicker chair where I sit during read alouds, morning meetings, and mini-lessons. Students also place completed work here. Next to my chair is a mini wicker chair that we call our "share chair"; it is used for a variety of purposes. For instance, my students take turns sitting in the share chair to help me demonstrate a mini-lesson, share something they wrote, or display special objects, such as a lost tooth or object for the math museum. The chairs foster a sense of community and pride.

—Allyson D.

Homey Touch

The pillow and bear on my chair give it a homey touch. Next to my chair is a table where I keep books for read aloud. I also have a wire basket where children place lunch forms, letters, or notices.

—*Chrissy K.*

Versatile Stool

I have a spare stool that I store under the easel. It's another optional place to sit. Nobody sits on my chair—that's my rule. But when we're doing publishing celebrations, kids can sit on the stool to share their work. Sometimes my student teacher sits here. Sometimes I'll even sit there to teach.

—*Orange G.*

Author's Chair and a Comfy Couch

We often have authors come in to share their work. They sit on the author's chair and the kids ask them questions or share their comments. Sometimes if there's more than one author, they sit on the couch together. The couch is also free for kids to sit on in the afternoon. The couch is like a homey, safe place for them to be in, and the children like it.

—*Jackie S.*

Tables, Chairs, and Other Furniture

"The arrangement of classroom furniture and materials helps determine the type of teaching that will take place there. "

— RONIT M. WRUBEL (2002)

STUDENTS' TABLES AND CHAIRS

The way you arrange your classroom reflects the way you teach. In classrooms where students are encouraged to work collaboratively in small groups, tables may be pushed together in clusters where children can sit around and help each other. Teachers who prefer to do direct instruction may position their tables in a traditional U configuration so everyone can easily see the board and the teacher. Take a look at how some teachers applied these ideas in their classrooms.

Community Builders

I group my students' double desks into clusters to promote partnership and small group work. I then create a U shape with all the desk clusters located next to our meeting area so that students are able to see the charts we created and the materials we studied during our mini-lessons. I prefer the U shape of desks because it takes up less space, allows for a variety of groupings, and creates a cozy area. Since students sit together in groups of four, they have the support of other classmates when needed. I like these double desks because while appearing like tables, each has storage space for students to store their materials, such as journals, book bags, and pencil boxes. This makes our transitions from one activity to another smooth and efficient.

—Allyson D.

For Faster Transitions

Last year, I pushed my tables together so kids could sit in small groups. But when I started test prep I rearranged the tables into the traditional U layout. I was using the overhead all the time and I needed everyone to see. With the old layout, many backs were turned to the board and it was very hard to do direct teaching. The U formation works. I've never had transitions this fast. Kids move from their desks to the meeting area inside the U in no time at all.

—*Barbara R.*

Lined Up for Space

I have a couple of tables in the middle of the room next to the meeting area. I also have several desks lined up against the wall where children can work individually. I have a small room so I'm confined by the geography of the room. I have to modify what I might do in optimum situations to accommodate the space.

—*Isabel B.*

The Size Is Right

My fifth graders are much bigger than, say, third graders, so they need furniture that's closer to adult size. I lucked out—I'm the only room that has these large tables and chairs in fifth grade. The kids feel more mature and so they behave accordingly.

—*Bari F.*

Signs on a Can

I turned old coffee cans into reusable sign holders with a little plaster of paris, a stick, and a clothespin. At the beginning of the year, signs listed the children's first names. As the year progressed and children moved around the classroom, the signs would change. I have listed last names, birthdays, phone numbers, addresses, and so on. My goal is to help children identify themselves in different ways.

—*Sally C.*

Homey Table

I have this little table at a corner next to the window where a kid might sit and read. One of my students made that lamp for me as a wedding present. She made it from scratch and it works. I was very impressed. The whole table setup adds to the room's homey feeling. I have a few extra tables like this around the room where kids can sit.

—*Bari F.*

Numbers for Math, Colors for Writing

I use playing cards for table numbers—I have tables 1, 2, 3, 4, and 5. The table numbers indicate the math groups. This year, I also color-coded the tables. Each card is held in place by a different-colored tape. The colors indicate the writing workshop groups so I have the red group, green group, and so on.

—*Miki J.*

Table Labels That Teach

I labeled my five tables using the five boroughs in New York City—Manhattan, Queens, Brooklyn, the Bronx, and Staten Island. We study the history of New York in social studies so we'll be learning about its five boroughs. I thought it would be neat to have kids grouped by the five boroughs. It helps me with transitions when I call kids by boroughs to come to the rug or to line up or get their coats and lunches.

—*Jennifer C.*

"Time Out" Table

I have this table next to the door that holds records of my kids' work. Kids wrote some short poems, which I compiled into a book. I also have albums of pictures from past years. This is a good place for a child who is having a hard day, who can't seem to fit in or can't do the work, or is upset about something. I send them here to take a break until I can talk to them. I'll say, "Go, take a time out at the table," and they know that it doesn't mean a punishment. A time out can also be a deep breath and a chance to reassess yourself. They all need it; I need it.

—*Jackie S.*

Seating and Storage Combined

These benches are made out of milk crates and a piece of plywood attached by cable ties. Every year, we have our students paint and design the benches. Kids sit on them during independent reading and at the listening center. They also keep their stuff in there—writing folders, math folders, writing notebooks, poetry notebooks— anything that might go in a desk. We have five benches, one for each table. They're in different parts of the room because there tends to be mass chaos of clustering when everybody has to get their writing folder. With the benches spread out, the kids are not all plowing into one area.

—*Jill S. and Jennifer G.*

Chairs With Pockets

All my students' chairs have these cloth covers with pockets at the back. I cut out the cloth and took them to the dry cleaner, who sewed them for me. In the morning when kids come in, they unpack all their necessities—their poem notebook and their plastic bag with their reading books in it—and slip them into the chairs' back pocket. This way, everything they need is within easy access.

—*Suk A.*

ALTERNATIVES TO THE TEACHER'S TABLE

Many teachers have dispensed of the teacher table because they are constantly moving around the classroom, providing support and instruction where they're most needed. But teachers still need a place for conferring and for storing paperwork and supplies. Here are some ideas:

Easy Retrieval
This is my little work station. I have a portable stereo here for playing classical music during writing. This is where I place things that I constantly retrieve, like dismissal forms and notes from the office, as well as work that I need to get done now, like papers to photocopy. Whatever I'm going to need for the day, I always have on this desk so when I'm teaching, I can just quickly pick it up.

—*Jennifer C.*

Observation Desk
This little table is where I pile my stuff. I'm rarely here except during reading conferences. When I do my meeting conferences, I try to get the message to kids that they're private and personal. If no one needs help and kids are just working in groups, I'll sit at my little table and observe. Sometimes I'll take a pad with me and take notes for my assessment.

—*Jodi G.*

My "No Interrupting" Table

In my classroom, I have several small round tables, each of which has a distinct purpose. My students know that my "no interrupting table," shown above, is where I do many of my reading and writing conferences. When I am conferring with a student, other students know they shouldn't interrupt unless it's an emergency. Another small table I have is the red "hot table" (*at right*), which stands next to my classroom entrance door. Any notes from students, parents, or the office are placed here.

—*Allyson D.*

Organizing Supplies

"In arranging learning materials, the goal is to make them as accessible as possible and to encourage students to use them independently and responsibly."

—MARLYNN K. CLAYTON (2001)

How you organize supplies will depend on whether you want them to be easily accessible to children or out of their reach. If you want to foster independence in children, place supplies in a communal area within their reach and at their eye level. Clearly label all supplies with words and graphics to help students return everything to its proper place. Supplies that you want to keep in your control should be stored inside a closet or on high shelves. Make sure children understand which supplies they can use and which ones they can't.

Cubby in a Tub

Each child in my class has a plastic tub, which is his or her own cubby. Inside their cubbies are their own personal supplies, like special pens or markers or pencils. They keep their reading journals and reading logs/folders in there as well as their theme-study notebook. The cubbies help kids keep organized. They help keep the room a lot neater.

—*Jodi G.*

Room Divider

My supply shelves divide my room into two areas—on one side is the meeting area, on the other side are the tables and work area. There's easy access around the supply area so that during cleanup time, children are able to quickly put away their colored pencils and rulers and whatever else they were using. Kids can easily access either side of the shelves so they can reach over if they have to.

—*Jen H.*

Organizing Odds and Ends

This shelf holds odds and ends that I use often for measuring or whatever we're doing in science. The illustrated labels on the bins help kids find what they need.

—Jen H.

Easy-to-Reach Supplies

I have an open-topped shelf where I keep supplies. The kids know where books and supplies are in my room, and they can reach them. This way, they have access to everything that I have.

—Jackie S.

See-Through Supplies Sorter

I worked on my closet the week before school started. I found this plastic shoe caddy and it helps me get organized. I use markers a lot so I like that the see-through pockets let me sort them by colors and access them easily.

—*Jennifer C.*

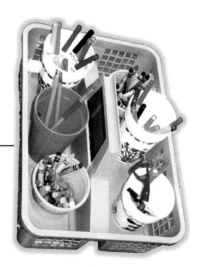

Supplies Caddy

Every table has one of these plastic baskets with supplies. Supplies are communal—everyone shares the same things. At the beginning of the year, I give my students a supply list. When they bring in their pencils, crayons, markers, and so on, I sort them into cups and place them in these baskets.

—*Suk A.*

Labels, Labels Everywhere

Every shelf and cabinet in this room is basically labeled. Not only do the kids have to be independent, but so do all my extra people. I have student teachers, "America Reads" tutors, and other people who come in. I don't want to be constantly telling them where everything is. It may be a little bit over the top, but at least it leads to independence.

—*Barbara R.*

OTHER FURNITURE

Sometimes a classroom needs more than just tables, chairs, and shelves. Unexpected furniture, such as a clothes rack or a toy mailbox, can add personality to your room as well as serve a practical purpose. See some examples below.

"All About Me" Shelf

I think this wicker shelf is a reflection of me. It has photos of important people in my life, my family. The cookie jar is something that I remember my kindergarten teacher had so I had to have one in my classroom. These are just some beautiful things that I've collected through the years, some from kids, some from teachers. It helps children see me as a person, not just their teacher.

—Chrissy K.

Postal Central

We do a big post office study every year. We use this mailbox outside our classroom, and people mail us letters. Our class is in charge of delivering the mail to the whole entire school. The mailbox is just a way of getting kids very excited about our postal unit.

—Chrissy K.

In the photo (on signs): Rhymin Simon, Schedule Shark, Courageous Cow, Our Puppets

Puppet Holder

Marilu walked by a clothing store that was going out of business and she saw this rack. A true visionary, she imagined that it could be a place for our puppets. We taped pencils to the side of the rack so they can hold up our puppets.

—*Edgar M. and Marilu P.*

Classroom Library

" ... think of the library in your room as the *heart* of effective literacy instruction. "
— D. RAY REUTZEL AND PARKER C. FAWSON (2002)

LIBRARIES AS TEACHING PARTNERS

According to Reutzel and Fawson (2002), the classroom library serves five major functions: to support literacy instruction, to help students learn about books, to provide a central location for classroom resources, to provide opportunities for independent reading and curricular extensions, and to serve as a place for students to talk about and interact with books.

As you will see, some teachers put their library front and center, making it the focus of their classroom. Others set aside a special corner for their library, where students can enjoy some quiet reading time. Either way, the idea is to entice children and foster their love of reading.

Library Centerpiece
The library is the most important part of the room. I want it to be the first thing people see when they enter so that they understand that literacy is a very important part of this classroom. I think the way I organized my library—with the clearly labeled baskets and nice, comfortable rug next to the shelves—is inviting to children and makes them want to sit down and read the books.
—*Naomi L.*

Little Library Nooks

I stacked up some shelves to save space and to create a little barrier to make this truly a library area. The sofa separates the library from the rest of the room. The pillows, which my grandmother made, usually go on the carpet to make extra "library spots." During independent reading kids can sit down and really enjoy reading—it's kind of like little library nooks.

—*Jennifer C.*

Couch Potatoes

This is our reading and library area, separated from the meeting area by one of the bookshelves. I also have a couch, where three children can sit during library time each day. This helps them relax and be a little more comfortable while reading. I have a seating system called "Couch Potatoes," which is similar to "Pillow People" (see page 18). There are also "Past" and "Future" cups, so the "Couch Potatoes" change every day.

—*Jodi G.*

Easing Congestion

Most classroom libraries are contained in one area. I decided to have my library in three separate places. Series books are along the windows, books sorted by authors are near my computer center, and books separated by genre are next to the coat closets. When my students are browsing in the library—for example, if six people are looking for books at the same time—they're not all crowded in one area. It's less claustrophobic.

—*Stephanie S.*

Great Reading Expectations

It's always nice when kids walk into a room and the first thing they see is the library. My kids' lives are so surrounded by reading; they love to read. When they come into the room they see all these books that are organized by author and by genre—science fiction, fantasy, historical fiction, and so on. It gives them a feeling that reading is the expectation and it's going to be a big part of their school life.

—*Miki J.*

ORGANIZING AND LABELING BOOKS

A typical classroom library contains a variety of books, both fiction and nonfiction, leveled for readers of different abilities. The way you set up, organize, and label your library can help students make better, more appropriate book selections (Reutzel and Fawson, 2002). It also helps students return books to the right place, saving you time and keeping the area neat.

Sticker System

I am a science teacher. I want my library to mimic regular classrooms' libraries so it's a natural transition for kids when they come into my room for science. In addition to clearly illustrating each basket's label, I put matching color stickers on the label and on the books inside the basket. Kids can then match up the color of the book back to its basket. So if they're not sure, for example, if a penguin is a bird or a mammal, the color stickers can guide them to put a penguin book back in the bird basket. The colored sticker system makes it easy for all of us.

—Jen H.

Script Labels

All the labels in my library are printed in a script font. I changed it from last year when my students were in fourth grade. Now they're in fifth grade, and they're learning script.

—Miki J.

Labels That Last

My library is clearly labeled so children know what level and what author they can choose from. The basket labels are color-coded—I have all the series books in yellow, all author books in pink, and all genres in green. I typed the labels on my computer and brought them to a store to get them laminated. It may be more expensive, but the store does hard laminating, and hopefully the labels will last. I place a small white sticker with the reading level in the corner of each basket's label to make it easier for children to choose "just right" books.

—Barbara R.

MATCHING BOOKS TO READERS

Many classroom libraries have a separate section of leveled books, where each book bin might be labeled from A to J, for example. Most of first-grade teacher Chrissy Koukiotis's library is leveled. She divided her library into three sections, identifiable only by color:

" The blue bins are for the emergent group—kids who are reading books from kindergarten or books that are really simple. The yellow section is for kids who can read more words on the page and are able to do it more independently. The red bins are for more fluent readers. Kids know which section they belong to. I tell them, 'This is a good section for you right now.' I wouldn't want to hurt anybody's feelings by telling them, 'These are for you because they're easy,' or 'You're emergent.' I know that when kids choose books, they'll make better choices for themselves because most of the books are on their level. And I've carefully chosen which books I want in each basket, and I know all the books that are in the library. So when kids go and choose books, it's not just random choosing; they're making smart choices because I've scaffolded it for them. **"**

Author on Display

The books on this display shelf are ones that we are focusing on in our author study. For example, right now, we're studying Ezra Jack Keats. This makes it easy for kids to come up and compare his different books.

—Chrissy K.

No Labels

These book baskets are in order of difficulty, but I don't label anything. I don't believe in labeling; I believe in learning about your environment. We don't label everything in our house. We just know where everything is after a while. It's part of the learning. I point out to kids, "The easier books are there. The more difficult books are up here. Some of the favorites like the Berenstain Bears are there." I don't have to write that this bin is Roald Dahl, because kids will find it eventually.

—Jackie S.

Potpourri Library

Along one side of our meeting area is my "potpourri library." My classroom is filled with baskets of books that are organized by reading level, topic, genre, author, and so on. I think, however, that it is also important to have a shelf filled with a mixture of books that range in reading level, genre, and topic so that students can practice selecting books. I spend several mini-lessons demonstrating how to tell if a book is too hard, too easy, or just right, and invite students to practice selecting books in the potpourri library. This prepares students to choose books at the bookstore and library.

—Allyson D.

ADDING SPECIAL TOUCHES TO THE LIBRARY

A comfortable couch, a basket for special books, personalized sign-out cards—all these enhance an already special place and encourage children to become more active participants in the library.

Special Black Couch
The black couch in our library is a ripped-up old thing, but it's perfect. It's easy to clean because it's vinyl. And I bought pillows and a rug. The kids can lay down on the couch or on the rug, or take the pillows and lay down with them. I play classical music, and the library becomes very peaceful.

—*Orange G.*

Lost Books—Found
When children would put back the books in the library, occasionally they would forget where the books go. Sometimes I encourage them to ask their friends or myself. Most of the time, I have them put the "lost" book in this bin labeled "Books Looking for a Home." The librarian for the week takes the books in the bin and puts them back in the correct baskets.

—*Jennifer C.*

Cozy Reading Area
We have a little couch area next to the library where I keep baskets of magazines and books. All the books that I've read aloud go on the display case so kids don't have to find them in the library. The books on the coffee table are small copies of big books that we've read. Kids sit in the couch area to read in the morning when they're browsing or after they finish their reading activities.

—*Suk A.*

Yummy Stories

I inherited this picnic basket from one of the teachers before he left. Inside, I put "nutritious stories"—picture books that kids might look through to give them ideas about their writing.

—*Miki J.*

Library Books to Go

I placed a blue crate in our entrance hallway. The kids place their school library books there so that when we go to the school library, one of the kids can just pick up the crate and carry it to the library. It's right near the door.

—*Miki J.*

Expert Big Books

We ordered this special storage container for our Big Books. The students are very familiar with all the books in here because we've used them in shared reading. They've become "experts" at reading these books, and they love taking them out to read during reading time.

— *Edgar M. and Marilu P.*

Sign-Out Card Reminders

I put library card pockets, one for each kid, on this cabinet next to the library. When kids borrow a book from our library, they write the title on an index card, which goes in the pocket. Then, when they come in the next morning, they cross off the title. It's basically a routine to help them remember to take a book home every night and to take it out of their school bags in the morning.

—*Chrissy K.*

Classroom Displays

"Classroom displays that celebrate students' efforts and have a connection to the daily life of the classroom are one of the most powerful— and overlooked—tools for teaching. **"**

—MARLYNN K. CLAYTON (2001)

On the first day of school, many classrooms keep displays to a minimum. An alphabet frieze may be displayed above the chalkboard and a welcome sign posted on the door, but for the most part, walls and bulletin boards are bare, except for perhaps some brightly colored paper covers. One teacher explained why: The walls are ready for kids' work to be displayed during the first week of school. The very first assignment kids work on is a "getting to know you" project—it could be a self-portrait, a poem, or even a personal time line. When the kids are done, their work goes up on the walls. This is just one way of letting kids know that this is their classroom and that they matter here. Find out what other kinds of displays convey the same message.

"Getting to Know You" Door Display
This is something we did at the beginning of the year. The kids decorated their own paper dolls and I brought fabric from home. That's when I shared that my mom sews and that she has so much fabric at home. Working together on this door display was a way of getting to know my kids and them getting to know me. Now we have something beautiful to put on our door.
—*Chrissy K.*

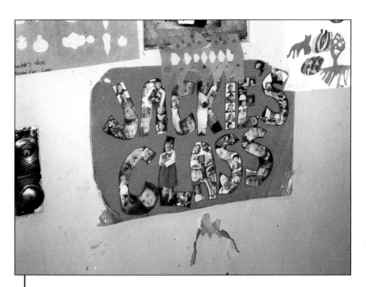

Kids on Display

At the beginning of the year, my door is bare except for this sign saying "Jackie's class." This is made up of pictures that I cut out from magazines. As the year progresses, I add kids' work, such as poetry or pictures, on the door. When parents come in, they see right away what their children have done.

—*Jackie S.*

New York City's Finest

I put up pictures of my kids on the door under the heading "New York City's Finest." At the beginning of the year, we talked about community, so I wanted my kids to feel like they were a welcome part of the class.

—*Naomi L.*

Class News Word Wall

Every morning we, as a class, think about what's going on for the day or something special that has happened. We then write the class news and post it on these boards. I usually keep the news up for a little while because I want the kids to use it as a word study wall. During writing, if they need a word that they remember we used on Wednesday's class news, they can just come up here and find it.

—*Chrissy K.*

Family Newsletter

My students work on our family newsletter every Friday. If a student did something exceptional for the day or for the week, I encourage him or her to write about it. Three students design the newsletter each week. My goal is to have everyone participate in it at least once. We send the newsletter home every Friday and post a copy on the door for everyone to read.

—*Stephanie S.*

Tooth Chart to Promote Independence

I have a chart for when kids lose a tooth. The bag underneath contains extra teeth, and it's really accessible to kids. This chart also helps kids be more independent. When they lose a tooth, they take a tooth out of the bag, write their name on it, and then post it up on the chart—all by themselves.

—*Chrissy K.*

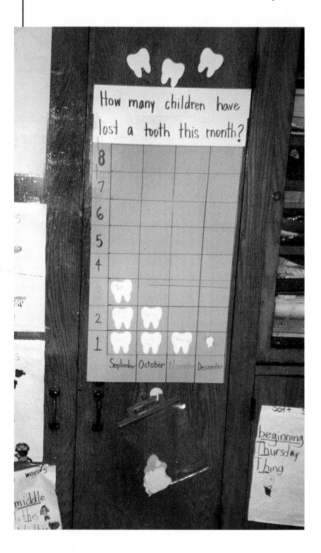

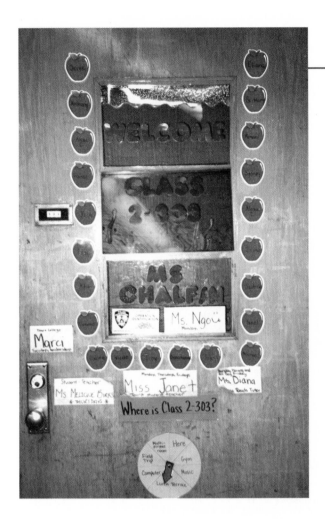

Who's Who in This Class

Anyone coming to my classroom knows exactly where they are and who is in this class. This includes all the different student teachers and tutors that help on different days. It's also exciting for the children to have their names on the door. When they line up, they get to find their names. The spinner shows visitors where we are, so if we're not here, they know where to find us.

—Jennifer C.

Quilt to Show Unity

Our class made this "peace quilt" in remembrance of September 11. The quilt format emphasizes the sense of unity between the teachers and our students. This is especially important during that difficult time at the beginning of the year when our students are first getting to know us. We placed the quilt outside our room in the hallway because it exemplifies excellent work that the class has done as a whole.

— Allison G. and Janice K.

CHAPTER 2

CREATING
Classroom Routines & Procedures

> **"** Routines are the backbone of daily classroom life. They facilitate teaching and learning…. Routines don't just make your life easier, they save valuable class-room time. And what's most important, efficient routines make it easier for students to learn and achieve more. **"**
>
> — LINDA SHALAWAY (1998)

When routines and procedures are carefully taught, modeled, and established in the classroom, children know what's expected of them and how to do certain things on their own. Having these predictable patterns in place allows teachers to spend more time in meaningful instruction. This chapter presents routines and procedures teachers have used to help them successfully manage important times of the school day, including arrival, transitions, and dismissal.

Arriving in the Morning

> **"**Prime time in school is the first few moments in a class. If you blow these moments, you blow the impression, the sale, and the success of a class.**"**

— HARRY K. WONG (1998)

As children start trickling into the classroom, they need to know exactly what to do. What should they do with their homework? Where should they put their book bags? Where do their coats and other materials belong? What should they do while they wait for the rest of the class to arrive? When does class actually start? When kids know the answers to these questions, they can move smoothly through the morning routine and get straight into learning.

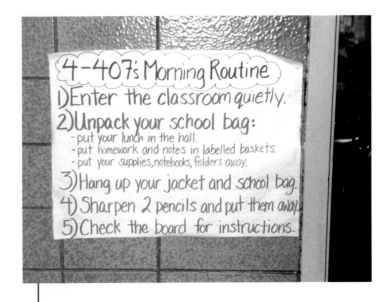

Morning To Do List

I post my morning routine outside the class so kids know what to do before they enter the room. They know to put their homework and notes in my baskets labeled "For Homework" and "Notes for Orange." Then they put their stuff away, sharpen their pencils, and do their "Do Now" activity, which is usually a quick math problem. At 8:25 A.M., we meet at the rug for morning meeting.

—Orange G.

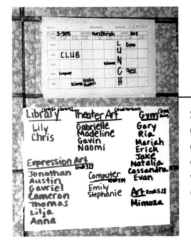

Schedule Reminder

Our students go to self-selected clubs first thing in the morning once a week. We make a list of who belongs in what club to remind students where to go that morning. We also post our class schedule outside the classroom so parents and colleagues know what we're doing and when. It also acts as a reminder for parents; for example, if they see that tomorrow is gym day, they'll remember to dress their child appropriately in sneakers.

— Allison G. and Janice K.

Welcome Table

We have a small table outside the classroom for notes, messages, and any other things that kids need to take home to their parents. In the morning, kids drop off their homework in the basket. We also have a dry-erase board that we use to write morning reminders, like "Go to Science."

—*Jill S. and Jennifer G.*

Visual Morning Reminder

We have a "Good Morning" chart right by the door that lists everything students need to do when they come in. The chart uses both pictures and words. Students have a lot of responsibilities in the morning —take off their coats, give us notes, put their folders away, and sign in. They can look at the chart and check to see that they've done everything. This helps them become more independent.

—*Edgar M. and Marilu P.*

Literacy-Building Sign-in Sheets

I have clipboards where kids sign in when they arrive in the morning. There are three clipboards so three kids can sign in at the same time. At the beginning of the year, I list children's first names and have them rewrite their names next to it. Each month I change what the kids have to write. In November, they write their first and last names; in December, their initials. In the second half of the year, kids write words from the word wall, opposite words, compound words, and so on.

—*Isabel B.*

PUTTING AWAY BOOK BAGS AND COATS

As soon as students enter the classroom, they need to deal with their stuff. They need to know where to stow their book bags, lunch sacks, coats, and other personal belongings—and do it right away. Some classrooms are equipped with closets, making it easy to keep things organized, out of sight, and out of the way. Others have cubbies with hooks for hanging up stuff. Whichever setup you have, establishing a routine for hanging up book bags and coats can help children get themselves organized.

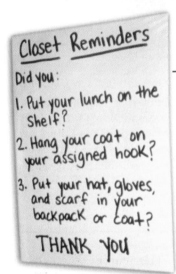

Closet Reminder
Our closet space is very small, but everything is labeled. I posted a closet reminder so kids know to put their lunch on the shelves and to hang up their coats, hats, and gloves in the winter.

—Jennifer C.

Alphabetical Hooks
We don't really have a closet for kids' coats and bags. We have cubbies with hooks that I've labeled with the kids' names in alphabetical order. The shelf space above the hooks is also clearly labeled—that's where their lunch boxes and hats and scarves go. All this leads to kids' independence, which frees me up to do everything else.

—Isabel B.

Boys' and Girls' Closets
Last year, I labeled the closet hooks with kids' names so each kid was responsible for just his or her hook. But because some hooks were at the back of the closet, we had crowding issues. This year, I have about the same number of girls as boys, so I just made separate closets for girls and boys. Those who arrive first hang their coats and bags in the back hooks so those who come later don't have to push through other bags. Separating boys and girls works in this case. It's easy for me and it's easy for them.

—Orange G.

COLLECTING HOMEWORK AND NOTES

Setting up a system for turning in homework shows students how much you value their work and fosters independence and accountability. Assigning a place for students to put their homework and notes from home will help manage the flow of paper in the classroom.

Folders Ready for Homework

First thing in the morning, children are responsible for turning in their homework. They would go to the homework table, take out their homework and any signed notes and place it into the wire basket. Empty folders go in the plastic bin, ready to be filled with the next assignment.

—*Sally C.*

Training for Responsibility

I give a set of homework for the week on Mondays and collect it on Fridays. But kids still need to bring their homework folders home and back every day, because they get notices from school throughout the week. Every morning they put their homework folders in the basket and I check them for notes or permission slips. Then, in the afternoon, they pick up their folders before going home. It's a way of training kids for responsibility, independence, and organization.

— *Naomi L.*

Grade "A" Homework

Kids turn in their homework folders and notes in this area. I have a bin for homework I've already graded and another for ungraded homework. Our postal assistant hands back graded homework. During my prep period I go through kids' homework folders to make sure that they've taken home all the notes. I put notes in myself because my kids are only 7 years old and still need to be monitored. Later in the year as they grow more independent, I introduce mailboxes so they can get their own mail.

—*Jennifer C.*

TAKING ATTENDANCE AND DISPLAYING SCHEDULES

After the bustle of putting away book bags, coats, and homework, taking attendance and discussing the schedule can help bring students together and build community in the classroom.

Self Representations

When the students first started school we gave each one a precut cardboard figure. We then asked each student to decorate it to represent him or herself. Now, when they come in the morning, the children move their figures to the center panel to indicate that they're here. It's a very concrete way of doing attendance for kindergartners. We refer to our attendance chart not only during morning meeting but also during math, when we might use it to teach number sense, addition, subtraction, or one-to-one correspondence.

— *Edgar M. and Marilu P.*

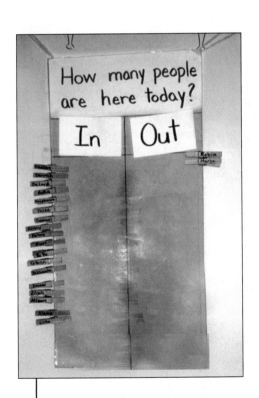

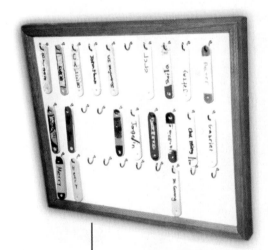

"In" and "Out" Pins

When kids finish unpacking their stuff, they go to the attendance chart. The chart is on the opposite side of the room away from the closets so there's less overcrowding. Kids move their labeled clothespins from "Out" to "In." During attendance, we bring the chart to the meeting area and look at how many pins are in and how many are out. At the end of the day, someone moves all the pins back to "Out."

— *Suk A.*

Attendance Tags

These are my kids' in/out tags. My dad drilled hooks into this picture frame and shaped the name tags from scrap wood. The kids decorated their own tags. I use this setup to take attendance. When kids enter the room, they get their tags from a cup and hang them on the hooks.

— *Renee H.*

Morning Rhythm

Every morning, I assign one child to be the "teacher of the day." When we take attendance, the "teacher of the day" takes down the drum and, as I read children's names, he or she taps each name's syllables on the drum. For example, say I read the name Zachary Johnson. It would be *tap-tap-tap tap-tap*. I mark the attendance, then the "teacher of the day" takes it to the office.

—Isabel B.

Clock Schedule

In second grade, kids need to know how to tell time. At the beginning of the year, they know *o'clock* and *:30*. When we talk about the day's schedule during morning meeting, I move the hands on the clock next to each thing that we're doing. For example, shared reading is at 9:30 and independent reading is at 10:00. I try to schedule most of our lessons at the hour and half hour because it's easiest for kids at the beginning of the year. Later in the year, we do counting by 5s and I readjust the schedule.

—Naomi L.

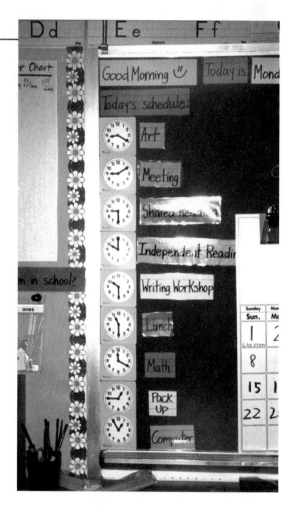

Illustrated Schedule for ELL Students

I have this set of schedule cards that we use every day. My schedule cards all have pictures that I got from a clip art program. I knew that some of my children might be English-language learners, and I wanted them to know the schedule even if they couldn't read the words. I laminated the cards so I could keep them for many years.

—Jennifer C.

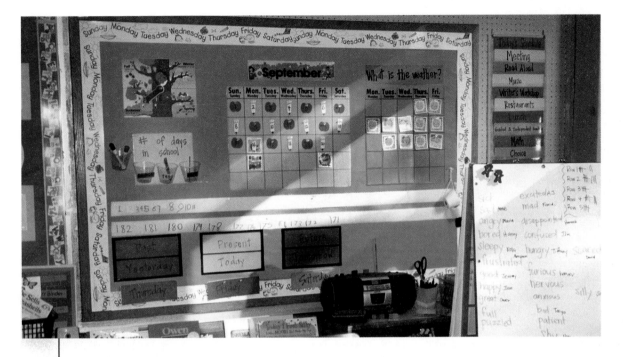

Learning-Rich Calendar

Children learn so much from ten minutes of calendar activities. We work on patterns using the numbers on the calendar. I write the numbers on precut templates and place them in a pattern for children to guess. We start with a simple ABAB pattern using pencil and apple templates, then move on to ABC, AABB, and so on. I change the pattern and templates each month. We also have two number lines—one that counts up (1,2,3…) and one that counts down (182, 181, 180…)—on rolls of calculator paper. It helps children see and understand that numbers don't just go one way. It is a simple introduction to subtraction and negative numbers. Then we use sticks to help us count up to the 100th day of school and beyond. The sticks will eventually get bundled into groups of tens and hundreds, helping children learn place value. Kids get a lot of math and organization in those ten minutes.

—Sally C.

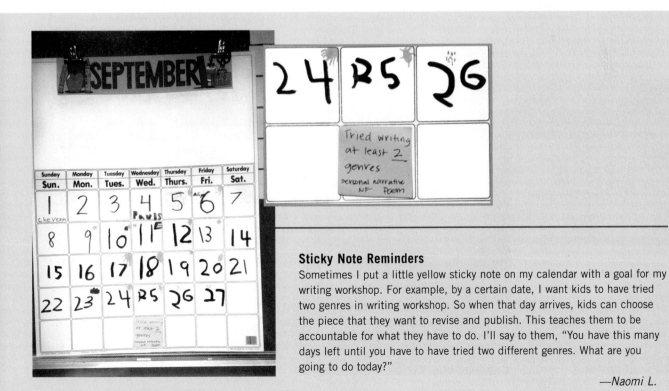

Sticky Note Reminders

Sometimes I put a little yellow sticky note on my calendar with a goal for my writing workshop. For example, by a certain date, I want kids to have tried two genres in writing workshop. So when that day arrives, kids can choose the piece that they want to revise and publish. This teaches them to be accountable for what they have to do. I'll say to them, "You have this many days left until you have to have tried two different genres. What are you going to do today?"

—Naomi L.

Throughout the Day

❝Don't ever ask children to do nothing. When children aren't sure what they are supposed to be doing or they are waiting for you to tell them what to do, they will come up with something to do, and in most cases, this will be something you don't particularly want them to do.**❞**

—DEBORAH DIFFILY AND CHARLOTTE SASSMAN (2004)

Students move through many activities during the course of a typical day, from whole-group lessons to small-group work, from reading time to math time, from in-class work to specials outside the classroom. It's important to plan for these in-between times just as carefully as you plan your lessons. With predictable routines in place, students can move smoothly from one activity to the next without losing learning time. The teachers in this section share some clever ideas for signaling transition times and keeping track of students as they leave the classroom for various reasons during the day.

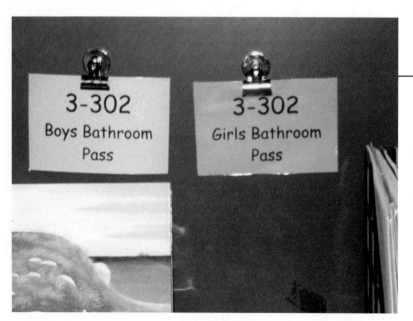

Ready-to-Go Passes
These are the boys' and girls' bathroom passes for when they go to the bathroom. They're hanging from magnetic clips on the board next to the door. Kids don't always have to ask to go. They see the pass and they take it. If it's not there, they can't go.
—*Barbara R.*

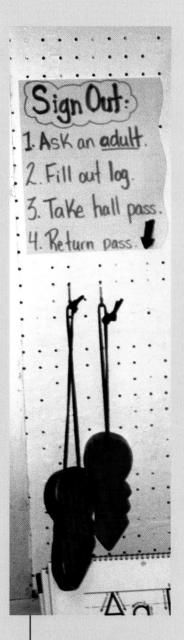

Visual Student Tracker

We have children who go to ELL (English-Language Learners), occupational therapy, physical therapy, counseling, and speech. We set up these little charts based on the different rooms that students go to, including the boys' bathroom and the girls' bathroom. At the bottom, we have the students' names on Velcro. The charts are at the children's level so they can move their own names when they leave the room. It's helpful to us because we always know where the students are. It's helpful to children because it reminds them where they're going. And it's helpful to the other students in the class because when someone is looking for a friend, he or she can come over here and see, "Oh, she's out of the class-room right now." It's basically a visual reminder.

—*Edgar M. and Marilu P.*

Time Management Sign-out Sheet

These wooden keys are my hall passes. Only two kids can be out at a time and kids can't be in the hall without a pass—it's school-wide policy. I also have a sign-out book under the passes. To help kids with time management, I have them write down what time they leave. Kids have to ask before they go basically because I want to know where they are.

—*Renee H.*

Transitions & Getting Children's Attention

Students, especially young ones, need gentle reminders to help them get ready to move from one activity to another. Developing routines for transition times helps students manage themselves and take responsibility for their learning. These ideas alert students to upcoming transitions and let them know how much time they have to clean up and get ready for the next event.

Shadow Clock

Many kindergartners cannot yet tell time and haven't grasped the concept of time. So we have a shadow clock that we use for transitions. We'd say, "There are five minutes left," and we turn the red shadow to the 5. The shadow moves by itself, and since five minutes is always the same, kids begin to understand how long five minutes is.

—*Edgar M. and Marilu P.*

Teaching Kids to Listen

I use this cowbell and toy telephone to get children's attention. Each of the keys on the phone produces a different tone. Sometimes I ask kids to mimic the sound so they learn to listen as well. I might also clap out a pattern and have them repeat it back to me. I also use silent gestures to signal for attention, such as putting one finger on my lips.

— *Jackie S.*

Musical Transitions

For one of our transitions, we do a countdown on the piano. We have the children visualize that we're in a rocket ship, and they have their seatbelts on when they're sitting and looking up at us. With piano music, we countdown to blastoff, "5, 4, 3, 2, 1." When we get to zero and blastoff, we will do a little space scanner music to see if everybody is in their seatbelts. If they're in their seatbelts, then we can blastoff to learn. It works!

—*Edgar M. and Marilu P.*

Leaving the Room as a Class

Teaching children how to line up and walk down the hallway in a quiet, orderly fashion is essential for safety and shows consideration for other classrooms. It also saves precious minutes. While you're out, it's helpful to let others know where you've gone. Teachers in this section share some simple techniques to keep kids on track in the hallways—and to help parents, administrators, and others find you if necessary.

Lining Up Made Easy

I have a little rubber "path" that goes from the meeting-area rug to the door. I've found that kids can't naturally line up in two straight lines, so I assigned them line spots and have them line up on their square—somebody stands on the C, another stands on the elephant, and so on. I assign the most responsible kids to lead the line and to bring up the rear. When you have the really responsible kids at each end, it just somehow helps everyone in the middle.

—Chrissy K.

Line Spots Where Kids Can Do Their Best

We have line spots in our class to allow each student to move around the school in the safest way possible. If there are two students who distract one another often, we will place them in opposite spots in line. If a child would do best standing near a teacher, we put him in the front of the line where he could be easily monitored by either one of us. We stress to our students that we want them all to do the best they can in school, and that is why some students may move line spots—because their old spot is no longer an area where they can do their best.

— Allison G. and Janice K.

Destination Known

When we leave the classroom to go to math or lunch or the gym, we change the destination sign at the door so people know where we are. At the back of the door is a pocket that holds cards for every place that we go. We have a "destination person for the week." Before we leave the classroom, the destination person takes out the correct card, sticks it to the door, and off we go.

—Suk A.

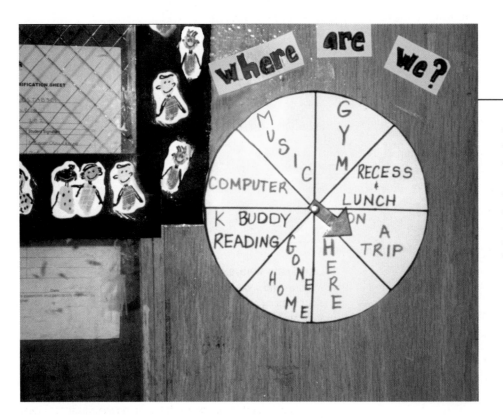

Where Are We? Wheel

The principal likes to know where we are, so when we leave the classroom, we just turn the dial on the wheel to show where we're going. It's also helpful for people who come to visit. They just know where we are right away.

—Barbara R.

Ending the Day

"Finally, don't forget about students as classroom helpers. Students can accomplish many of the tasks that adult volunteers do … the experience gives students the chance to be responsible and to be depended upon. These are important confidence- and character-building opportunities. "

—LINDA SHALAWAY (1998)

Just as a morning routine helps set the tone for the rest of the day, an end-of-the-day routine helps get children and the classroom ready for the next day. You may want to enlist some children's help in tidying up the classroom while others gather their belongings, including homework.

CLASS JOBS

Assigning jobs to students is a wonderful way to promote independence and teach children responsibility. Determine what tasks you want students to be responsible for at the beginning of the year, and try out one of the systems on the following pages to keep students employed all yearlong. Clearly defining a job, demonstrating its duties, and providing a written reminder of what's involved are essential steps for implementing job assignments.

Clear Job Descriptions

When I was setting up my classroom, I realized that there are certain things that I want to do for my kids and certain things that I want the children to be responsible for. I made enough jobs so that every kid in the class has a job for the week, except for two students who are substitutes and one child who is on vacation. If someone is not sure what his or her job is—let's say the closet inspector is not sure what to do with the closet—I have a "What Is My Job?" chart. Kids can read that the closet inspector closes the closet in the morning and opens it before lunch.

—*Jennifer C.*

Today's Jobs

Andrew
Angelo
Ava
Brianna
Caboose — Callie
Daniel
Diego
Lunch Boxes — Eli
Emily
Eric
Jade
Leader — Janna
Closet — Julia
Natalie
Olivia
Sonny
Messenger — Sophia
Summer
Messenger — Vladimir

Wanted—Peer Problem Solver

We have six rotating jobs in the classroom, most of them pretty self-explanatory. The "caboose" is somebody who brings up the back of the line. The caboose is also like a peer problem solver, so that if you need advice about how to solve a problem, you can go to the caboose and he or she might have an idea of how to solve it.

—*Edgar M. and Marilu P.*

Teacher's Elf

Everybody in my class has a job, and most of the jobs are standard. Then there's the Elf. The Elf is the person who helps me out the most. For example, when we're getting in line or walking down the hallway, the Elf walks up and down the line and makes sure everyone is quiet. Out in the yard when the bell rings, the Elf gets people in line before I get there. I got the idea for that job from my cooperating teacher; it's kind of like Santa's little helper. It feels like it's the most important job.

—*Miki J.*

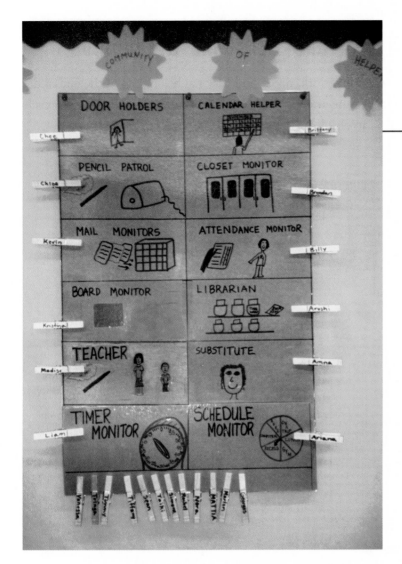

Real Jobs for Real Kids

I try to narrow down the jobs we need for our classroom. I want jobs that I know kids actually need to do and are useful to our community. It's also a management thing—you don't want to have too many kids up at the same time. About half of the kids—those whose pins are at the bottom—are on vacation. The clothespins rotate clockwise so everyone gets a chance to do all the jobs in the class. The clothespins are organized in alphabetical order for easier management. The best thing about the job chart is that it immediately helps kids take ownership of their classroom. The jobs are rotated on a weekly basis.

—Barbara R.

Permanent Jobs

Every child in my class has a job that keeps us all functioning. Kids keep the same job for the whole year. I hand out job applications at the beginning of the year and explain the expectations for each job. Then, each kid comes to me and says, "I'd like to apply for that job because . . .", and describes the reasons why. If their application is accepted, they get the job.

—Isabel B.

PICKING UP HOMEWORK, NOTICES, AND PERSONAL BELONGINGS

Most teachers I visited have a routine for picking up homework, notes, and personal belongings at the end of the day. Some teachers have class monitors that hand students their homework. Others distribute homework in each student's mailbox, giving students the responsibility to check their mailboxes before leaving for the day.

Shoe Bags for Mail

Shoe bags make great mailboxes for students. Copy paper fits nicely into each holder. I put students' homework and family notices here and they collect them at the end of the day. I call a few students to come up at a time so there's no crowding.

—Stephanie S.

Extra Homework Sheets for Absentees

My fifth graders are going into middle school next year, so I'm pushing them toward independence and self-sufficiency. I write the week's homework and when it's due on the board. The kids are responsible for copying down their homework on their own homework pad or the homework sheet that I made. I keep extra copies of homework sheets and notices next to the homework board. If kids are absent, it's their responsibility to look in here for homework sheets and notices that they missed.

—Miki J.

Double-Checking Homework and Mail

I put students' homework and notices in their mailboxes every day. Then I post every single paper that's in their mailbox on my homework board, which is next to the door. At the end of the day when kids get their mail, it's their responsibility to double check with the homework board to see how many pieces of mail they should have that day. If for some reason a student is missing a piece of mail, then he or she has to get an extra copy from me.

—Bari F.

HELPING STUDENTS ORGANIZE HOMEWORK

On the first day of school, first-grade teacher Sally Cho handed her students their own homework envelopes labeled with their names. She wanted her students to have something to take home right away. These plastic envelopes made homework special for kids:

> I bought colorful plastic envelopes for kids to carry their homework in. They are able to withstand a whole year's worth of travel. I snipped off the strings and replaced them with Velcro so they're easier for kids to open and close. Then I wrote each child's name on the front and they were ready to go.

Similarly, third-grade teacher Barbara Rossi got her students red plastic folders, which are more durable than regular paper folders. In addition, she created a homework assignment booklet for each child:

> I gave every kid in my class a homework assignment booklet where they can record their homework every day. On its cover, I listed resources for homework help and added a blank chart where kids can write their classmates' names and phone numbers in case they missed the homework. Kids are also given a colorful plastic bag to keep their reading books in.

Reading Bags to Go

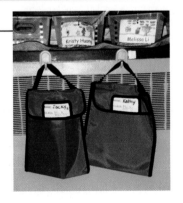

I found these really cute reading bags from a catalog last year and bought one for each of my students. Kids pick a book from their reading basket on top of the radiator every day and put it in their reading bag, which hangs on self-stick hooks on the radiator. Then they bring their reading bags home.

—Chrissy K.

Closet Line

When it's time to go home, kids pick up their reading bags, then line up behind this masking tape on the floor to get to the closet. For safety reasons, only one kid is allowed in the closet at a time. Usually the line isn't long because some kids might be signing out books, while others are waiting on line. If the line starts getting long and we have to leave, I stand next to the closet and say, "Okay, two at a time." But I keep an eye on them because they could get hurt in the closet.

—Chrissy K.

CHAPTER 3

ESTABLISHING
A Learning Environment

"When we create classroom environments that are attractive, comfortable, and purposeful, providing materials that support our work with children, structuring our time to support our goals, then we'll surely reap the results of our efforts. "

— SHARON TABERSKI (2000)

Once routines and procedures are firmly in place, teachers can spend more time doing what they do best—teaching. In classrooms I've visited, teachers have used every surface available to foster learning. Classrooms are often divided into sections or have learning centers devoted to specific content. Within each content area, walls, boards, the ceiling, bookshelves, tables—whatever is there—are put into service. The result is a learning-rich environment that supports students as they do their independent work. This chapter presents many of the creative ways teachers have enriched their classrooms to create stimulating learning environments.

Reading

> **"** If we want children to respond to books they've read in ways that will deepen their understanding, then we must provide the tools, opportunities, and demonstrations of how to do this. **"**

— SHARON TABERSKI (2000)

A survey conducted by Michael Pressley and associates (1996) found that "expert teachers presented their classrooms as places in which literacy development occurred throughout the day, connected both to formal curriculum and less formal activities." In addition to setting up a classroom library, teachers can do many other things to support their students' literacy learning, such as creating and displaying charts that help children pick "just right" books, or that show the features of nonfiction, or that remind children of their reading objectives. Teachers might also establish independent reading centers and set up a system for deciding who goes to which center. This section presents a sampling of the tools and techniques teachers use to promote reading in their classrooms.

Choosing "Just Right" Books

I teach my students how to choose "just right" books for their independent reading. I use the analogy of riding a bike (as illustrated in the posters above). Over the course of several mini-lessons, I demonstrate reading books that are too hard, too easy, and just right by role playing (with a great deal of exaggeration). I draw the bike analogy as well as record on each poster key phrases that help readers distinguish between books. I display these posters near our book baskets so students can use them as resources when selecting books.

—Allyson D.

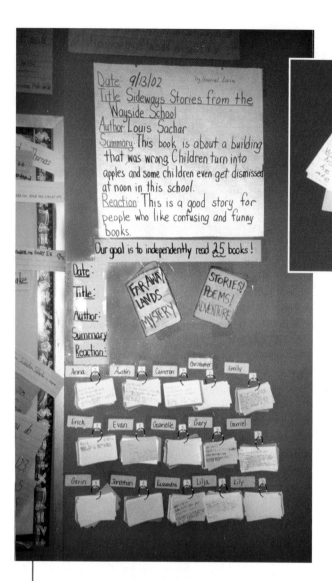

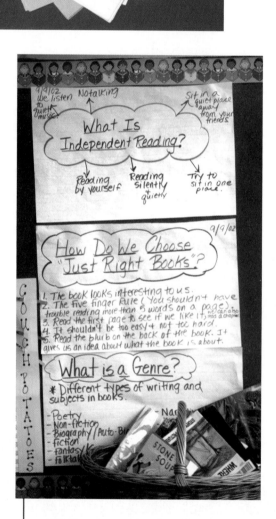

Color-Coded Reading Logs

In our school, third graders have to read at least 25 independent reading books. When kids finish reading a book, they record the book's title and author, the date they finished reading, and a brief response to the book on an index card. We wrote a sample entry on chart paper for kids to use as a model. Each child has a set of 25 index cards, five of each color, held together by a ring. The colors help kids keep track of how many books they've read. For example, when they've used up all the white cards, they know they've read five books; when they've used up the orange cards, they've read ten. We hang these "reading logs" on hooks behind the door.

—Allison G. and Janice K.

Reading Strategies Reminders

During a series of mini-lessons my students and I discuss various reading strategies, such as choosing books that are just right for them and distinguishing between different types of genre, as well as the kind of behavior I expect during independent reading. I model these strategies and write them on chart paper. Then I post these charts in our reading center next to the library so students can refer back to them as needed.

—Jodi G.

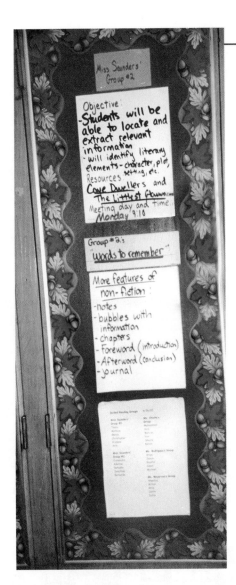

Reading Objectives on Display

I post my guided reading objectives from the very beginning of school, as well as the date and time each guided reading group meets with me. Each group may have a different objective. One group may be studying the features of nonfiction text while another may be working on making inferences. During each session, we list the big ideas behind the strategy we're focusing on.

—*Stephanie S.*

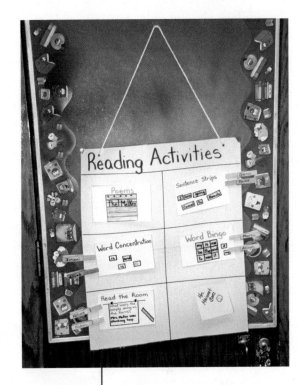

Reading Activities on Rotation

This is my reading activities chart. I have lots of different activities—"Read the Room," "Word Concentration," "Sound Concentration," "Sound Bingo," and so on. They're all based on my reading assessments. I change the activities around depending on what I think the kids need and to keep them interesting. I use Velcro to attach the activity cards to the chart. Kids look for their personalized clothespins to see which activity they're assigned to do.

—*Suk A.*

Traveling Literacy Center

This is my traveling word cart, where I keep all my literacy activities— magnetic letters, cookie trays, jigsaw sentence strips, chalkboards, games children can use during guided reading. It's basically a cabinet on wheels, so I can roll it out during guided reading or choice time.

—*Samantha K.*

KEEPING TRACK OF PUZZLE PIECES

First-grade teacher Suk Albino enhances her reading curriculum with various activities she created. For one activity, she wrote several sentence strips based on sentences the class had written together. She then cut each sentence strip apart and put the individual word cards in an envelope—one for each sentence. Students use the cards to reconstruct the sentence. Suk labeled each envelope with the sentence and a number in one corner. Each word card in an envelope has the same number written on the back. Why?

> **"** I got tired of kids saying, 'Ms. Albino, I found the word *my* on the floor.' I mean, how many sentences have the word *my* in it? Now, since each word card has a number on the back, I can easily determine that this card goes into the #5 envelope. I did the same thing for my sound puzzles. I have three bags of sound puzzles and each bag is designated 1, 2, or 3. So if a piece falls on the floor and we find it later, we know exactly which bag it goes into. Figuring out where missing pieces belong used to drive me crazy until I got smarter. **"**

Word-Study Envelopes

Under my word wall, there is a laminated envelope for each child's word-study words. Every Wednesday, I write five words that they will be studying for the week on 4"x6" index cards and place them in each envelope. Children work on a different activity each day. They may be building words with magnetic letters, making connections, or giving their buddy a practice test. At the beginning of the year, we all work on the same words. Eventually, the class will break into three or four different levels, based on assessment.

—*Sally C.*

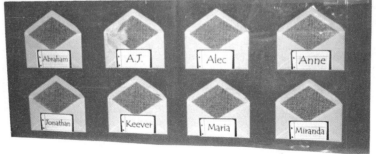

Word Masks and Highlighting Tape

I made these "word masks" in different sizes. When we're reading a poem, for example, I might ask some-one to come up and mask the word *friend*. Otherwise, some kids who are just learning English might think the letter *r* is *friend*, instead of the whole word. I can also flip the mask to find a chunk in a word, like /ee/. I also use highlighting tape. For example, if we're looking for chunks, we might highlight the chunks with different-colored tapes.

—*Suk A.*

Color-Coded Word Wall

Because I have kids from K to 5 in my science room, I color-coded my word wall. This way, kids can see right away which words they need to know. I don't use the word wall in the traditional way. With kindergarten and first grade, I'm not so insistent that they have the spelling right. For example, I put *camouflage* for kindergarten because we're studying insects. The kids know they can find the word here if they want to write it in their journals. In second, third, fourth, and fifth grades, students have to spell their words correctly.

—*Jen H.*

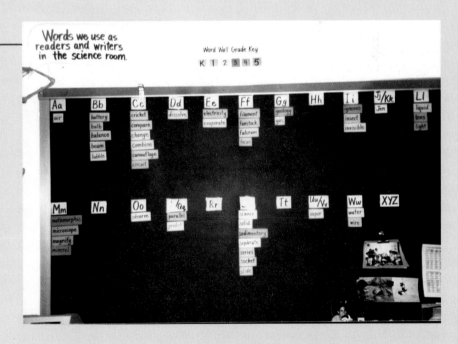

Backward Labels

For one of our word-study activities, children build words using magnetic letters on cookie sheets. Magnetic letters are stored in shallow plastic boxes with dividers. To help the children figure out where letter goes, I painted the letters backward at the bottom of each plastic box. That way, when children open the lid, they will see the letter the proper way.

—*Sally C.*

Easy Access Words

I placed my word wall on the closet doors near floor level. That way, the words are easily accessible to kids. I use Velcro to stick the words to the door so kids can go up to them and take off the word that they need for when they're writing or whatever.

—*Naomi L.*

Word Pockets

I bought this commercial alphabet display to use for my word wall. I stuck little library pockets—the kind that librarians use in books—behind the letters because I always had a hard time searching for words inside a plastic bag. As a teacher you always want to save time. So all the words that begin with *M*, for example, are right in the pocket behind the letter *M*. It's easy!

—*Chrissy K.*

Word Patterns

In our class, we try to address the needs of different types of learners. For example, in our word study we're doing the long /a/ sound. We try to get kids to notice patterns in words that have the long /a/ sound. For example, sometimes *ey* makes that /a/ sound, sometimes *a*, a consonant, and an *e* make that /a/ sound. Then we grouped the words according to these patterns, and wrote them on different color paper. It's really visual for kids so it helps them.

—*Allison G. and Janice K.*

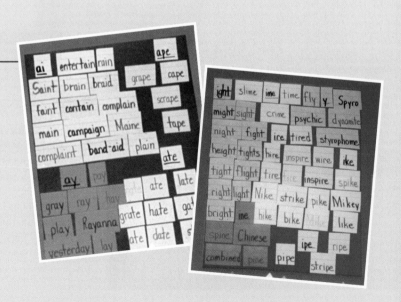

Dynamic Animal Groups

After I've assessed the children—to see what level they are at and what skills they need to work on—I divide them up into guided reading groups. I let the kids decide their group name. I told them it had to be an animal. Because they're only in first grade, I put each group's name with a picture of their animal. The kids' names are attached with Fun-Tak because the groups are dynamic. For example, maybe one day I notice that Kenny needs to work on something that another group is working on. He might spend some time in the other group for a while and then move back.

—*Suk A.*

Our Class Dictionary

After we complete a unit of word study, we collect all the words and add them to our Class Dictionary. I use rings to hold the chart papers together and hang the dictionary on a clothesline. When students need to find a word that they know we've already studied, they can just come up to the Class Dictionary and flip it open to find the word they need.

—*Stephanie S.*

Reading Spots

During independent reading, children choose special reading spots throughout the classroom. To help them remember where they sit and how many bodies can be at a certain area, I made this chart of our classroom—three children per table, six on the big rug, and two on the smaller rugs. Since reading spots change every few weeks, I laminated their names and attached Velcro to the back (and on the chart) so they are easy to move around. I keep the chart low so the children can move their names around, quickly and easily.

—*Sally C.*

Writing

> **"**Children come to school with an innate curiosity about writing.... We need to provide an environment in which the social and physical conditions promote writing.**"**
>
> — NANCY AREGLADO AND MARY DILL (1997)

The writing center is an important component of every classroom I visited, an area carefully designed to stimulate students' excitement about writing. It needs to be well-organized and well-stocked so students spend their time writing and not hunting for pencils and paper. The ideas in this section have been developed by veteran teachers in response to their students' needs and their own teaching goals. Read on for the efficient strategies they've devised to organize supplies, store student folders, display student work, and keep track of students' progress. Having these effective systems in place helps make writing time productive and fun.

Writing Central

The writing center is the most important area in our classroom because we use a lot of supplies in the center most of the day. I put the writing center in the middle of the room so that kids could easily get to it. That's also why I arranged the kids' tables around it.

—*Chrissy K.*

Mini Writing Center

I use this low table for my mini writing center. This way, everything is within reach for the children. I put out different paper choices for writing, which I've introduced slowly through the writing curriculum. We have colored pencils here and crayons and markers in the back, plus their writing folders. Kids can also choose to write on this table.

—Samantha K.

Paper Choices

This is my supply table for writing. I have precut construction paper for kids to use as book covers if they want to make their stories into books. I have four paper choices: One is a short horizontal with a box in which they can draw. It's for beginning writers, but can also be for more proficient writers when they decide to make books. There are three other kinds of paper with different amounts of space for drawing and writing. There's also extra drawing paper.

—Suk A.

Boys' and Girls' Writing Bins

I have two plastic bins where kids store their writing folders. The bins are labeled B for boys and G for girls. It's a much easier way for kids to find and store their folders.

—*Naomi L.*

Fun Erasers for Writing

This is how I keep track of where kids are in the writing process. I put up this corkboard and divided it into the different stages of writing. I bought a bunch of pencil erasers and gave one to each kid. I stuck the erasers onto pushpins and the kids move themselves through the writing process, depending on what they're doing. Some of the erasers were the same, so I got a marker and drew designs on them. Kids like them. They're fun!

—*Bari F.*

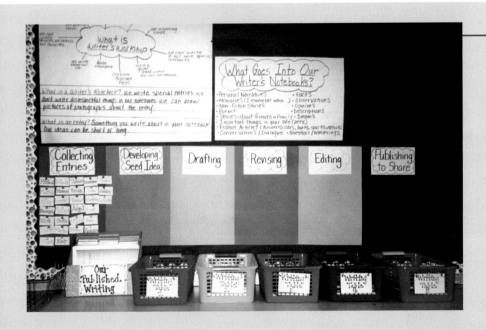

The Writing Process

Our writing program is based on Columbia University's Teachers College Reading and Writing Project. In our writing center, I have a display that shows the steps of the writing process and where each student is in the process. During our first writing cycle, I explain each step and model for students what they need to do at each step. Students have name cards that they can move as they progress through the cycle. I also have baskets—one for each table—where students store their writing folders and writer's notebooks. It's a way of keeping them all organized in one place.

—*Jodi G.*

WRITERS' LIBRARY

In addition to her classroom library, fifth-grade teacher Bari Fischer set aside a bookshelf filled with books that she uses for her writer's workshop. Many of her ideas come from Columbia University's Teachers College Reading and Writing Project:

" Most of the books here in my writing center are the ones that I use as my 'touchstone text,' meaning that I go back to them time and time again so kids would be very familiar with them. Kids need to be very familiar with certain stories in order to learn from them. It's hard to learn from something if you're trying to first understand it. So if they've heard a story a million times, then they can concentrate on the craft of the writing instead of trying to understand the story. They'd say, 'Oh yeah, we know the story,' and I respond, 'Great, because now we're going to focus on the writing part.' "

Bari's basket labels are very descriptive so students know exactly where to go for writing models, such as "Books That Help Make You a Better Writer" and "Poetry to Support Writers." A basket labeled "The Way Memories Are Contained in Bits of Life" holds books with one-page stories. "This basket is actually for memoirs, but those with little bits of life and little, tiny stories," explained Bari. "'How the Physical Things in Our Lives Hold Stories' is a very interesting collection about how an object can be so sentimental and can hold so many stories." Another basket labeled "Copies of Touchstones" is for kids to use when they're studying a writer's craft. Instead of taking the actual book, kids take one of the copies back to their seats and study how the writer was writing and get some ideas off of that.

"Edge of Your Seat" Stories

Before we study a genre or craft technique in writing, I read aloud several texts that exemplify the writing style. This open-faced bookshelf displays these touchstone texts that we read repeatedly and refer to during a study. When writing "edge of our seat" stories, for example, my students learn from our touchstone texts that writers stretch out the most important moments of stories (i.e., suspenseful, frightening, exciting moments) by using rich, descriptive language to record a character's dialogue, body movement, and internal thinking during the key moment.

—Allyson D.

Math, Poetry, Art, and More

"Ultimately, it is you the professional who decides what, where, when, and how to teach, keeping in mind the particular needs of your students. **"**

—LINDA SHALAWAY (1998)

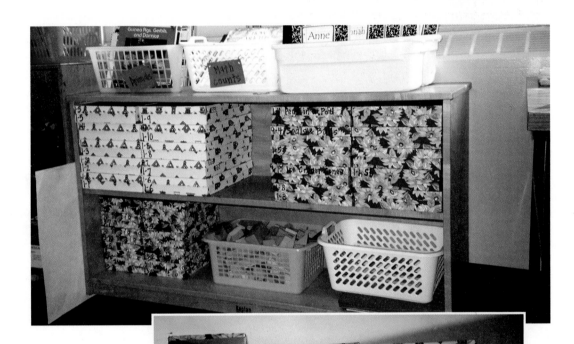

L iteracy is a primary focus in elementary classrooms, but content area subjects are also well represented. The following pages showcase inviting centers housing math, poetry, and art activities that help students practice important skills.

Math Centers in a Box

I made these math boxes to help children learn important skills in a fun way. There are 150 boxes with different learning activities, divided into three levels. After I've assessed the children, I place them into one of the three levels. They are allowed to work at their own pace. It is wonderful to see children excited about doing math. I've even had children ask me if they can work on math boxes during free choice.

—*Sally C.*

Leveled Math Games

To meet the needs of my students' various math abilities, I created a leveled library of math games to help them practice math skills. For students struggling with a math concept, I modify a grade-level game, label it with a red dot, and place it in the red bin. Once the students have moved past the emergent stage I direct them to choose a game from the orange bin, which contains games at grade level. For students who quickly master concepts and skills, I create games that provide more challenge and place them in the blue-dot bin. While students work in partnerships and small groups playing math games, I confer with them and use this assessment data to organize and teach small-group strategy lessons.

—Allyson D.

Time for Fractions

We were studying fractions, so I divided our clock into four sections to show quarters. It also helps kids who are still struggling with time at the fourth grade, as well as for kids who are ELL (English-Language Learners). The labels help them think of each number on the clock as a chunk of 5.

—Renee H.

Birthday Math

One of the things we study in math is how to collect and record data. We do a poll to find out how many children have birthdays in September, October, and so on. Then we look at different ways we might show that data. One way is to do a pie chart, as shown above.

— Naomi L.

Our Poetry Window

My poetry reading centers are designed to have students read, study, and practice a variety of poetry techniques. I organize the reading centers and necessary materials into labeled baskets, which I store next to my red table. During poetry centers, students choose a basket and move it to its designated space in the classroom. "Our Poetry Window" is an example of one poetry center. In this center, students are asked to look outside the window, record observations, and compose a poem based on something they saw.

—Allyson D.

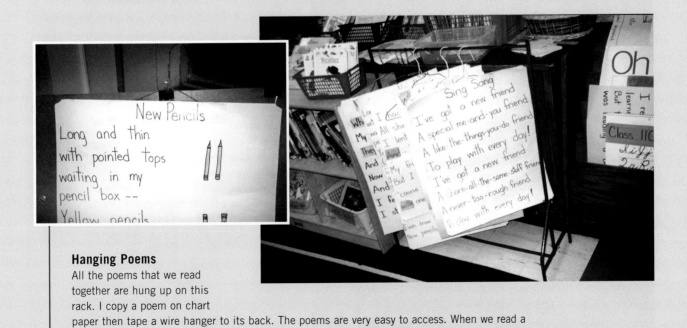

Hanging Poems

All the poems that we read together are hung up on this rack. I copy a poem on chart paper then tape a wire hanger to its back. The poems are very easy to access. When we read a poem together, I just take a hanger and balance it on a binder clip that I fasten to the easel.

—Suk A.

Easy Cleanup

I put our art supplies—paint, brushes, trays, and so on—near our sink area. The supplies are within kids' reach so they can get things for themselves. I have two children who are in charge of art cleanup and can easily wash the brushes and put them away after an art activity. Children can do many things on their own if you let them.

— *Samantha K.*

Free Art

Our art center is basically our free time center. When we have free time, the kids might make cards for people on their birthdays or make some crafts. We have yarn, sticks, construction paper, all kinds of art supplies that they can use. The kids set up the art center on their own so they know where everything belongs.

—*Chrissy K.*

Familiar Stories on Tape

This half-circle table serves as our listening center. I have small copies of shared reading books, which I read into tapes for kids to listen to during reading workshop. During reading workshop, I prefer that they reread familiar stuff. That way, they're not just listening—they're actively looking and reading along and noticing the words.

—*Suk A.*

Fluency-Building Tapes

I have a listening center where I have a bunch of Walkmans, which I bought at Target for $5 each. I posted rules up so kids know how to use the center. Kids still need a listening center in fourth grade. For example, some kids want to read Harry Potter but it's just too hard for them, so I get it on tape to encourage fluency. I also have a lot of ELL students who are struggling with English. One way I try to expose them to the sounds and print of the language is through books on tape. As they begin to say the words along with the tape, the students gain the confidence they need to develop their oral-language skills.

—*Renee H.*

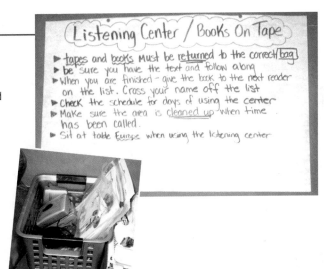

Reenergizing Activities

Every once in a while, I give kids ten-minute breaks in the afternoons so they can relax and get reenergized. I keep activities in this yellow bin that kids can pick from during break time. I find that kids can focus longer when they know that they will be given a break to play a game, draw, or chitchat with friends later in the day.

—*Renee H.*

Games Under Cover

I keep games on a shelf at a remote corner of the room. The games are for choice time once a week, so the shelf is not used every day like the math shelf or the supplies shelf. That's why it's out of the way. I fitted a rod into the shelf and made curtains to keep the games out of sight until it's time to take them out.

—Miki J.

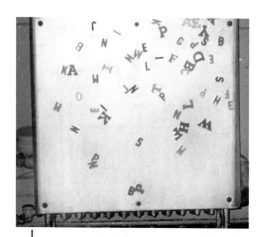

Magnetic Radiator

Kids use this radiator shield as their magnetic board during choice time. The shield protects the kids from the heat. New York City kids are used to radiators.

—Isabel B.

Blocks in a Bucket

Keeping my blocks in a bucket under the homework table saves lots of space and time. I started with them in a bookshelf, but it took too much time to clean up, especially when students had to organize each block onto its proper shelf. So instead, I put all the blocks into one large bucket and the kids clean up in no time.

—Sally C.

Building Is a Must

It would be very difficult for me to have an early childhood classroom without a block area. I need to see kids build. Once a week we have a captain of the block area who chooses the block team. On Thursdays, the block team puts away all the blocks. The front of the shelves has dark silhouettes of block shapes so kids know where the blocks go.

—Isabel B.

Management Helpers

❝Organizing materials and information is an art that cannot be easily taught because a person's organization system must take into account his or her style. **❞**

—BONNIE P. MURRAY (2002)

If you're like most teachers, you're on the go all day, from before the first bell rings to after the last bus leaves. To make the days go more smoothly, busy teachers developed the ideas shared in this section. By keeping materials you need frequently at your fingertips and knowing where everything else is, you save time and keep focused on your main task—teaching. Read on for some small ideas that can make a big difference.

Lists to Go

I have a cork strip on the side of the closet next to my door. There I post the fire drill procedure, my emergency list, our reading buddy list, and any other paperwork or information that I need immediate access to when we leave the classroom. For example, during a fire drill I take the procedure with me so I know right away where to go. If we're going on a field trip I bring the emergency list, which has all my students' contact information. These papers are pinned right by the door so I can quickly take what I need on our way out.

—*Jennifer C.*

Basket for Substitutes

This magnetic basket is for all of the important things that I have to remember: the procedure for exiting during a fire drill, the procedure for taking trips, the class list, a schedule of who goes where at what time. It also includes important memos from the school district. I often refer substitutes to this basket because they can really find everything in it that they need for a day.

—*Jackie S.*

Weekly Lesson Organizer

It's important for me to keep track of all my lesson plans, homework, and any other paperwork that I need for the week. So I keep a file organizer with a hanging folder for each day, Monday to Friday. Each folder has a section for read aloud, shared reading, writing workshop, guided reading, math, and homework. Come Wednesday, for example, I'll have everything I need in one place. If I have something for the following week, I store it in the back of the organizer.

—*Stephanie S.*

Student Portfolios Made Easy

I have a storage bin filled with file folders with each kid's name. I keep all their work in it. And then when I have parent/teacher conferences, I'll have each child's folder in front of me and I can talk about the work that's inside. This is the easiest thing for me right now. I can even have kids file their own work.

—*Barbara R.*

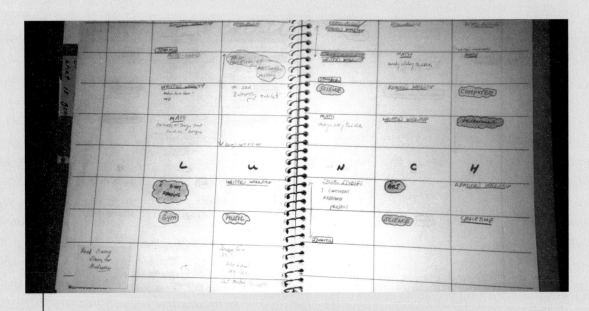

Color-Coded Lesson Plan

This year, I color-coded my lesson plan book, and it has helped me out a lot. For example, I can see how many times I have readers' workshop. It takes a little longer to write with different-colored pens, but I can see at a glance how many times I'm teaching math or when my preps are, for example. When I wasn't color-coding my lesson plan book, activities didn't really stand out.

—*Barbara R.*

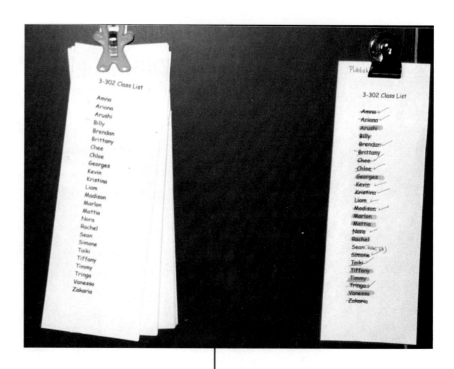

All-Purpose Class List

These are my class lists, which I use all the time for different things. For example, I might use one to check off who has turned in their permission slips, who hasn't published work, and so on. I use these daily.

—*Barbara R.*

Kids' Pins Chart

We use clothespins with kids' names on them for different things. For example, in our math curriculum we would do surveys. We would take a simple survey and kids would clip their pins on the survey chart based on their answers. But then when we would start working on another survey, the pins would still be on the old chart and kids would have to scramble looking for their pins. So I made up another chart just for the pins. Now kids move their pins right back to their names so that they're ready to use for the next day's survey.

—*Chrissy K.*

File Central

I don't have a desk in the classroom, so I feed off of my file cabinet. I keep things in here that I need, like book levels, extra math booklets, staff lists, student teacher work, and other things that I don't keep in my plan book. On the bottom, I have portfolios for all my students, as well as notes from home. I keep personal items on top of the file cabinet, like my picture from pre-K. The kids laugh when they see it.

—Jennifer C.

CHAPTER 4

Managing Behavior

> **"A classroom environment that is welcoming, accepting, calm, caring, and safe, a community where children enjoy success, feel understood, and respect each other, can go a long way toward influencing behavior. "**
>
> — ADELE M. BRODKIN, Ph.D. (2001)

Children need support and guidance in learning how to behave appropriately in the classroom. When children know how to behave properly they get along and work with each other better. Invest time early in the school year teaching and reinforcing appropriate behavior to help prevent problems later on. In this section, learn what some teachers do to manage their students' behavior, as a class and individually.

The Whole Class

> **"Classroom management is a major factor in helping children meet their potential."**
>
> — RONIT WRUBEL (2002)

Helping twenty or more students stay focused on learning tasks can be a challenge even for the most experienced teacher. Establishing rules and guidelines for acceptable behavior not only creates a safe learning environment for students, but it also helps you focus more on teaching rather than on correcting behavior. Consider involving students in developing rules to give them a sense of ownership and strengthen the classroom community. In this section, find out more about how some teachers establish rules with their students and use class incentives.

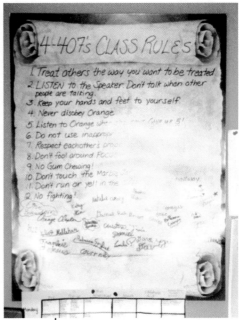

Five Is Enough

I have only five rules, and I always write them with my kids. If you have too many rules, they just become too overwhelming. My rules are always in a positive tone; they're never "Don't do this" or "Don't do that." I ask my kids, "What things should we do? We should keep our bodies to ourselves. We should listen when other people are talking," and so on. I think rules are important, but they don't need to be the focus of the room. So I put our rules at the back of the room. If I need to remind kids about a rule, I can always point to it.

—Naomi L.

Rules for the Class by the Class

My class made the rules on the second day of school. I divided the class into groups, and each group brainstormed some rules that we should have. When they were done, the class came together to share the rules and I listed the ones we agreed on. We read all the rules together, and then everyone signed them. If anyone or anything gets out of hand, I bring over the rules and we all read them together again as a reminder.

—Orange G.

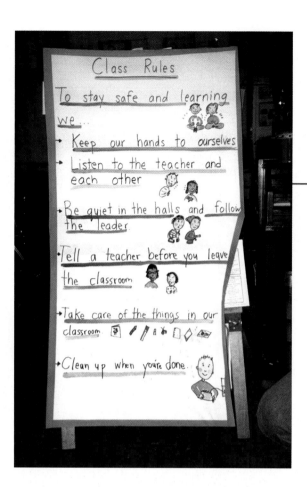

Clear and Meaningful Rules

Our class rules change every year, depending on the language that children come up with. We try to word the rules from a positive angle, but that's not always the clearest language. If it's more meaningful for children to say, "Don't talk in the hallway," we don't shy away from writing that. The most important thing for us is that the rules are clear, meaningful, and the children understand them.

—*Edgar M. and Marilu P.*

Class Incentive

The Magic Marble Jar is a class incentive—the class works together to earn marbles. At the beginning of the year when the jar was empty, I had students estimate how many marbles it would take to fill the Magic Marble Jar. Then I posted up their estimates. So it worked out as a math activity.

The class as a whole earns a marble for following class rules. Sometimes, if I get a compliment from another teacher about how my class behaves, I might reward them with a marble. We recently had a fire drill and my students got right on line, walked very well and very quietly in the halls, and they knew what to do. They got a compliment from our assistant principal. So after the fire drill, I also complimented them and I added a marble to the jar. When the jar is full, we might have a class pizza party.

—*Jodi G.*

VISUAL REMINDERS THAT HELP KIDS KNOW WHAT TO DO

Edgar McIntosh and Marilu Peck know how important visual reminders are for students. They created several charts that help children learn how to solve their problems independently and behave in class.

"We have a problem-solver chart that's visual. We tell children, 'If someone is bothering you, you can think of different solutions.' Together with the students, we brainstorm all things they can do before they even need to talk to a teacher.

Another visual chart we have is the RED chart. We call our meeting times 'RED light' times. With many children, when you say, 'Sit,' they don't really internalize that and think, 'Okay, that means I'm supposed to sit still.' So we have these three pictures and we go over them. R is for 'ready position', E is for 'eyes and ears'—and that means looking at the teacher or the board—and D is for 'do raise your hand.' The visual cue helps children really understand what you're asking them to do. Some students need help making these pictures in their heads. "

Road Rules

For their collaborative classroom, second-grade teachers Jill Simon and Jennifer Gillespie adapted a behavior management system that is based on traffic lights:

How To Stay On Green
2-310's Road Rules

Listen to the teacher STILL Listening / Quiet listening

Respect each other play nice games / tell the truth

Raise your hand Shhh

Keep your body to yourself hands-feet loud voice

Help your friends

Do your best work Try your hardest

Use kind words bragging 😊

Take care of our room

"First, we make the rules together with the class at the beginning of the year. When children come in the morning, everybody starts out with a green circle because they're doing the right thing. Like the traffic light, green stands for "go, keep doing what you're doing." If a kid does something that goes against one of our rules, we'll say, "You need to slow down and think. You're not making a good choice." If that happens three times repeatedly, we'll say, "You need to change to yellow so that you remember to slow down and think about what you're doing." The child then has to switch his circle to yellow. If the misbehavior continues, we'll say, "You really didn't change what you were doing. Now you need to stop. You need to change what you're doing and you need to make a different choice." And then the child has to change his circle to red.

Yippee!! Yippee!! Yippee!! Yippee!!

You have driven
1 MILE.

Yippee!! Yippee!! Yippee!! Yippee!!

If a kid stays on green all day, we give him a piece of paper that says, "Yippee! You've driven a mile." And when a kid collects 25 miles, we let him pick a treasure from our treasure box. Parents donate little toys, like party favors. If a kid turns her card to yellow, she doesn't get a mile but she doesn't get anything taken away either. And clearly, if a kid is at red, he doesn't get a mile either.

There is an incentive to stay on yellow. At the end of the day, we count how many kids have green and yellow circles. And then we tally it up in our "Weekly Goal." If most kids stay on green and yellow all week, we give the class some free time at the end of the week.

So green is like your personal incentive—to collect miles and get a treasure. Yellow, you're still helping the class to get choice time. And if you get a red, the whole class probably won't get a choice time on Friday. 〞

Individual Behavior Management

❝Inevitably, there are individual children who require more guidance than other children. Once again, we look on these situations as opportunities to help the misbehaving child internalize self-control.**❞**

— DEBORAH DIFFILY AND CHARLOTTE SASSMAN (2004)

Sometimes even a child with the best intentions has problems controlling him or herself and needs your help getting back on track. Rather than involving the whole class in dealing with one child's misbehavior, you may want to take the child aside and privately discuss his or her conduct. Depending on the child or the behavior, you may even want to include the parents or a guidance counselor in the discussion. See what two teachers have done to help individual students make good decisions about their behavior.

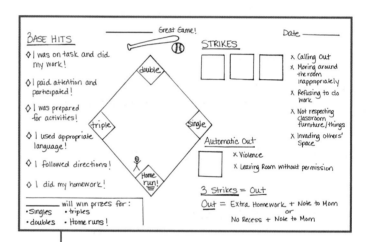

Personalized Behavior Modification

When I have a student with behavioral issues, I may create a special behavior modification chart just for him. One that I've designed with our school psychologist is set up like a baseball field. It keeps track of the student's positive and negative behaviors throughout the day. For example, at the beginning of the day, if he does something that's really easy for him, like using appropriate language, I'd say, "Great! First half hour of the day and you already have a single." He takes the sheet and colors in the first base. On the other hand, if he calls out, he gets a strike. As with baseball, three strikes and he's out. He gets an automatic out if he shows any violence or leaves the room without permission. If he gets an automatic out, he gets extra homework and a note to Mom, or no recess and a note to Mom. If he gets a home run—he does four good things in one day—then he gets a prize. Even if he gets just a single, he still gets a prize. There are levels of prizes.

—*Stephanie S.*

I'm Getting My Work Done!

Name: _____   Week of _____

	Monday	Tuesday	Wednesday	Thursday	Friday
Morning					
Afternoon					

My goal this week is _____ stars. If I reach my goal I get to choose an activity from the Surprise Box at home.

This week I earned _____ stars!

Individual Modifications

In every classroom there are usually a few students who struggle to get their work completed or who have behavioral issues. To help motivate students with these difficulties, I create individualized plans. The chart above is one I used with a student who was unable to complete his independent work throughout the day. I met with the student and his mother to explain the plan. I divided each school day into morning and afternoon. If the student was able to finish his work in the morning and/or afternoon he would earn a star in the corresponding box. Before beginning each week, I would set a goal (i.e., number of stars the student would attempt to earn) and record it on the sheet. (When beginning a plan like this I purposely set the goal low so students will be able to easily achieve it.) At the end of each week the student would count the number of stars earned and take it home to share with his parents. At home the parents and student created a "surprise box" that contained slips of paper naming special treats the student would receive if he met his goal. Rather than have material rewards, I encouraged the family to include things like staying up 15 minutes later at bedtime, being read a second read aloud, and so on. After the student was able to meet his goal for three consecutive weeks, I increased it. The ultimate goal was for the student to develop enough stamina to complete his work independently.

I used a similar chart for a student who continually called out during mini-lessons and whole class discussions. I created a chart that separated each day by subject area and used the stars and goals system. For students who have more serious behavioral issues, I use a daily take-home journal where I record both a chart and anecdotal notes of the student's behavior. Each night the journal goes home and is read and signed by the parent. This is an efficient way to communicate with the parents on a daily basis and hear their feedback as well.

—Allyson D.

Bibliography

Areglado, Nancy, and Mary Dill. *Let's Write*. New York: Scholastic, 1997.

Brodkin, Adele M. *Fresh Approaches to Working With Problematic Behavior*. New York: Scholastic, 2001.

Brophy, Jere, and Thomas Good. *Looking in Classrooms*. New York: HarperCollins, 1984.

Clayton, Marlynn K., with Mary Beth Forton. *Classroom Spaces That Work*. Greenfield, MA: Northeast Foundation for Children, 2001.

Diffily, Deborah, and Charlotte Sassman. *Teaching Effective Classroom Routines*. New York: Scholastic, 2004.

Murray, Bonnie P. *The New Teacher's Complete Sourcebook: Grades K–4*. New York: Scholastic, 2002.

Pressley, Michael, Joan Rankin, and Linda Yokoi. "A survey of instructional practices of primary teachers nominated as effective in promoting literacy." *Elementary School Journal*, 96, 363–384.

Reutzel, D. Ray, and Parker C. Fawson. *Your Classroom Library: New Ways to Give It More Teaching Power*. New York: Scholastic, 2002.

Shalaway, Linda. *Learning to Teach … not just for beginners*. New York: Scholastic, 1998.

Taberski, Sharon. *On Solid Ground: Strategies for Teaching Reading K–3*. Portsmouth, NH: Heinemann, 2000.

Wong, Harry K., and Rosemary T. Wong. *The First Days of School*. Mountain View, CA: Harry K. Wong Publications, Inc., 1998.

Wrubel, Ronit M. *Great Grouping Strategies*. New York: Scholastic, 2002.